# Rosa Parks
# BEYOND THE BUS
## Life, Lessons, and Leadership

H. H. LEONARDS

*Foreword by*
*Bishop Vashti Murphy McKenzie*

**R.H. BOYD**
EST. 1896
R.H. Boyd Publishing Corporation
Nashville, Tennessee

# Rosa Parks Beyond the Bus
*Life, Lessons, and Leadership*

Copyright © 2022 by H. H. Leonards

Cover and Page Design by Ken Strickland

Cover copyright ©2022, R.H. Boyd Publishing Corporation

The scanning, uploading, and distribution of this book without permission is a theft of the author's intellectual property. If you would like permission to use material from this book (other than for review purposes), please contact the Publications Division (*submissions@rhboyd.com*). Thank you for supporting the author's rights.

The publisher is not responsible for websites (or their content) that are not owned by the publisher.

Excerpts from *Dear Mrs. Parks: A Dialogue with Today's Youth*, by Gregory J. Reed, copyright ©1997, are used by permission of Lee and Low publishers.

Excerpts from *Rosa Parks: My Story*, by Rosa Parks and Jim Haskins, copyright ©1999, are used by permission of Puffin Books.

Images from the Library of Congress are from the Rosa Parks Collection.

R.H. Boyd Publishing Corporation
6717 Centennial Blvd.
Nashville, Tennessee 37209
*www.rhboyd.com*

Facebook/Twitter/Instagram: @rhboydco
First Edition: June 2022

ISBN: 979-8-88635-045-6

Printed in the United States of America

Note: Many of the photographs and documents appearing in this book are available for viewing online as part of the Rosa Parks Collection at the Library of Congress website (*loc.gov*).

## Praise for *Rosa Parks Beyond the Bus*

*The Mansion was Mrs. Parks' home-away-from-home where I visited with her many, many times. Like the 80-plus secret doors there, leading to stunning rooms throughout The Mansion, Mrs. Leonards' book opens doors into the innermost thoughts of Mrs. Parks—sometimes sad, sometimes joyful, but always insightful.*

The Reverend Jesse Jackson
American Activist

• • • • • •

*Like hidden doorways at The Mansion on O Street, there are whispered life lessons scattered throughout this poignant and powerful sharing of H. Leonards' friendship with a very human American saint, Mrs. Rosa Parks.*

Paul Williams
Academy and Grammy Award-winning Songwriter
ASCAP President and Recovery Advocate

• • • • • •

*In* Beyond the Bus, *H. Leonards peels back the layers of documentation on the life and journeys of Mrs. Rosa Parks by sharing firsthand experiences with Mrs. Parks, her friend and mentor, making this book not only a story, but also an essential item in the toolkits of today's social justice warriors who remain dedicated to moving the needle forward.*

Diem Jones
Executive Director/Co-founder
Voices of Our Nations Arts Foundation

• • • • • •

*The lens of history allows us to zoom into the people, places and movements of the past to bring the present into focus. Rosa Parks' legacy of advocacy and compassion inspires all who learn of her strength, dignity, compassion, and warmth—traits that are as vital today as ever. Thank you to H. Leonards, a friend and confidante to Mrs. Parks, for sharing the full picture of this quiet giant. Mrs. Parks' lessons in leadership are more important now than ever."*

Greg Harris
President/CEO, Rock and Roll Hall of Fame & Museum

## Dedication

This book is lovingly dedicated to the memory of Mrs. Rosa Parks; her mother, Leona McCauley; her loving husband, Raymond A. Parks; and Mr. Willis Edwards, her longtime friend, advisor, and advocate.

It is also dedicated to Davie Heck, the soul of the O Museum in The Mansion, and Steve Goldman, who lived directly across the street from me and was my confidant and pro bono lawyer for forty-two years. Both men are sitting with Mrs. Parks and Brother Willis Edwards right now, as they did on so many afternoons when they were all together, at The Mansion.

True love does survive. Perhaps, it's the only thing that does.

## Acknowledgments

I am so grateful to Luis Clavell and Susan Reyburn from the Library of Congress, who have been a beacon of light, strength, and hope; to renowned historian Dr. Douglas Brinkley who co-wrote Mrs. Parks' autobiography, *Rosa Parks: A Life,* and has given me enormous encouragement during the times we met, talked on the phone, and emailed; to Gary Tobin, who has been the patient captain of this project; to my wonderful, protective son, Z Stein, who grew up knowing Mrs. Parks during his formative and most impressionable years; and Tracy Halliday, who has been my backbone and confidante.

Special recognition and heartfelt appreciation are extended to Dr. LaDonna Boyd, Rev. Olivia M. Cloud, and Emmanuel LeGrair of R.H. Boyd Publishing Corporation, who deeply understand the spirit and power of love conveyed through the written word.

I also want to thank Howard Buffett. Through his largesse and generosity, many of Mrs. Parks' papers were donated to the Library of Congress and made accessible to the world online and in Washington, D.C. His gift has been a godsend.

Most of all, this book is dedicated to my loving husband, Ted Spero. Since we married, Ted has been everywhere in this journey with me and is my everything. He witnessed firsthand all that has transpired since our union in 2001.

Without the help of these committed souls, I could not have written this book.

*No copyright infringement is intended.*

H. H. Leonards

*"The Struggle Continues.
The Struggle Continues.
The Struggle Continues."*

Written by Mrs. Parks on a brown paper bag during the Detroit Riots in 1968.

(Photo: Mrs. Parks in African attire speaking during Pathways to Freedom, sponsored by the Rosa and Raymond Parks Institute for Self-Development, Library of Congress)

## Contents

From the Publisher, xi

Editor's Reflections, xii

Foreword by Bishop Vashti Murphy McKenzie, xiii

Prologue, xix

Accept Life's Gifts, 29

Integrity=Conforming Character to Reality, 33

Love Is All that Matters, 36

A Powerful Legacy, 41

Authenticity, 43

"Mother Parks", 44

"Mrs. Parksisms", 47

To Tell the Truth, 48

The Spirituality of Hope, 54

"Can Do" and "Yes" Are Magic Words, 58

Life Is a Jigsaw Puzzle: Eventually, Everything Fits, 63

Building a Loving Community, 64

Memories of Her Mother, 65

There Are Many Ways to Climb a Mountain, 67

It's All Good, 69

The Little Yellow School Bus, 72

The Assault: What Really Happened, 75

Mrs. Parks' "Room", 77

Coming Back Stronger, 79

The Art of Wielding Influence, 81

Trust Is Greater Than Love,   84

A Channel for Good,   87

Life Lessons,   89

Become Her Messenger...She Would Like That,   92

Author to Author...Friend to Friend,   94

Lost and Found: Faith, Patience, and Endurance,   96

A Family of Grand Ladies,   99

Tea Parties and Lessons in Grace,   101

Understanding May Come Slowly,   102

Quiet Strength,   104

Mrs. Rosa Parks and OutKast,   105

The Rebuke,   106

A Passion for Baseball,   108

Her Golden Rules,   109

The Jack of Hearts,   111

Proverbs,   111

Gospel Brunch Sundays,   114

Coming Full Circle,   116

The Remarkable Human Will,   119

Mrs. Parks' Struggle for Social Justice,   121

"I Love You",   129

Mrs. Parks and Nelson Mandela,   130

Taking Care of Little Things,   132

Keep the End in Mind,   133

Live a Positive Life,   134

Grace Supersedes Karma,   137

Dreams Transform Reality,   138

Learn Positive Lessons from Everything,   141

She Had to Help,   144

Forgiveness Is a Gift,   147

Meeting Pope John Paul II,   147

The Journey Home,   153

State of the Union Address,   153

The Presidential Medal of Freedom,   155

The Congressional Medal of Honor,   157

Knowing the Difference,   158

And Then, She Was Gone,   159

Mrs. Parks' Four Funerals,   161

Mrs. Parks' Safehouse,   170

Advisor to Young and Old,   170

The People Important to Mrs. Parks,   172

Going to Church with Mrs. Parks,   174

The Library of Congress Collection and Exhibition,   176

Back to Detroit,   178

Revisiting Detroit Two Years Later,   181

Change Has to Come,   183

The Story Continues,   185

Disciples Never Die,   186

About the Author (In Her Own Words),   188

Endnotes,   192

Resources Cited,   194

**Knowledge or Is it Acknowledgment?**

*"Memories of our lives,
our works,
and our deeds
will continue in others."*

Mrs. Rosa Parks

## From the Publisher

Heralded as the Mother of the Civil Rights Movement, the life and legacy of Mrs. Rosa Parks reaches beyond generational, racial, and economic divides.

Her wisdom, faith, and love for people are what has made her legacy endure since that brave day on a Montgomery bus in 1955. R.H. Boyd is honored to be the publisher for this book, and it is our hope that the lessons encapsulated between these covers will spark curiosity and bravery in current and future generations. Our stories and histories are intertwined—focused on the betterment of community through empowering Black voices.

It is not easy to stand up for what is right. In the example of Mrs. Parks, it is also not easy to sit down for what is right. By keeping her seat, she stood for honor, decency, and equality.

We are thankful that Mrs. H. H. Leonards trusted us to bring her story to life. Through her lived experience, she introduces untold stories and further engraves the legacy of Mrs. Parks in perpetuity.

*Rosa Parks Beyond the Bus* is a story of social justice, leadership, friendship, memories, hope, legacy, relationship woes, afternoon tea, faith, beautiful hats, an impressive shoe collection, and so much more. It is our hope that you enjoy this journey and are inspired by it to write your own story.

Onward,

Dr. LaDonna Boyd
Fifth-generation President/CEO
R.H. Boyd Family of Companies

## Editor's Reflections

In this beautiful book of memories, author H. H. Leonards indeed shows us Mrs. Rosa Parks beyond her Montgomery bus notoriety. In crafting this labor of love, Mrs. Leonards honors her mother-friend while helping readers to understand how Mrs. Parks was born and bred to take a stand by keeping her seat and saying, "No more."

Mrs. Leonards' word pictures are enhanced by the visual depictions gleaned from her personal collection, as well as those from the Rosa Parks Collection at the Library of Congress and other repositories that have cataloged the life of Mrs. Parks. Our work in compiling this book was greatly enhanced by the LOC collection, made possible by the generosity of the Howard G. Buffett Foundation.

Readers may notice that some of the images are a bit blurred or not taken at the best angle. Many of the photographs were taken for personal enjoyment and were never intended to be published. These imperfections add to the book's authenticity in sharing Mrs. Parks with the world.

From the day I reviewed Mrs. Leonards' manuscript, I believed her stories about Mrs. Parks could teach valuable lessons in civility. Mrs. Parks never allowed her sorrows or her joys to dictate how she related to others. In her lifetime, she experienced deep hurts, but she maintained a loving attitude toward humanity in the true spirit of *agape*.

She loved children and never hindered them from coming to greet her. She loved people and worked diligently to let love guide her decisions and actions.

Mrs. Parks is one of the most famous names of the twentieth century. Nevertheless, she remained humble, never using her renown for personal gain.

It is our collective hope that you will enjoy reading Mrs. Leonards' very personal stories about this amazing woman who blessed many lives, including her own.

Rev. Olivia M. Cloud

# Foreword

It is imperative to know when to stand and when to sit, when to speak and when to remain silent, or when to include and when to deny. Timing is everything.

At just the right time, Mrs. Rosa Parks chose to sit down so that others could stand with dignity. At just the right time, Mrs. H. H. Leonards opened the door of welcome to provide a resting place for Mrs. Parks in the winter season of her storied life.

Hebrews 13:2 (NRSV) advises: "Do not neglect to show hospitality to strangers, for by doing that some have entertained angels without knowing it."

When Mrs. H. H. Leonards said yes to Brother Willis' request for free lodging at The Mansion on O Street, she became the embodiment of this biblical directive.

Mrs. Leonards unknowingly extended hospitality to an angel of the Civil Rights Movement. Unaware of Mrs. Parks' identity and renown, she opened her doors and her heart to extend love to a frail older woman who was in great need of a loving shelter of safety. As Mrs. Leonards opened her front door, the physically fragile creature who entered concealed the greatness and strength that lay within one of the most pivotal personalities of the 20th century.

Thank God, there is something embedded deep down in the souls of the faithful that keeps responding to the Truth: that we are created in the image of God, that no single ethnic group, community, or country is above another in the sight of God.

The stories in *Rosa Parks Beyond the Bus* are confirmation that human beings can rise above cultural stereotyping based on hue and hair to live heaven's truth and contribute substantively to the body of work of our ancestors so that others may benefit from our sitting down to rise up at critical times.

It is little wonder that these two women bonded. Both women pioneered despite the odds against them. Neither stepped forward

Mrs. Parks and others walking down the aisle of Mother Bethel AME Church in Philadelphia, possibly during a Pathways to Freedom program, an initiative of the Rosa and Raymond Parks Institute, 1995. (Photo: Library of Congress, ppmsca.47437)

Mrs. Parks' family life revolved around Mount Zion African Methodist Episcopal Church in Montgomery, where her father's brother-in-law, Reverend Julius I. Dominick, was the pastor. Sunday church service was followed by daily prayers and devotional readings from the Bible. Because she grew up deeply rooted in the church, Mrs. Parks developed a strong faith that inspired her activism and assured her of triumph over her adversities, which prepared her for the trials ahead.

with the intention of making history, yet each, through simple determination, established something much larger than themselves—Mrs. Parks sparked a movement and Mrs. Leonards sparked the business enterprise that embraced her when her body was too battered to even stand for herself. I would dare say that both their experiences are the embodiment of "A woman's gotta do what a woman's gotta do."

Mrs. Parks' very being defied the lies of what culture and society have said about women of color, that destiny has consigned us to making beds we can't afford to sleep in, cooking food that others will eat, cleaning what others made dirty, or mending what others have torn apart.

Early in life, Mrs. Parks had determined she would do none of those things to earn a living. Her work at the NAACP Montgomery Branch and deliberate investigations of the sexual assaults against Black women in the Deep South affirmed her desire to make a difference in the lives of others. She was engaged in bold work that could even be considered dangerous, but she couldn't ignore what was happening to Black women every day and what had almost happened to her. This woman did what she had to do.

When a woman's gotta do what a woman's gotta do, she is sometimes able to sit down at just the right time to spark a movement. She'll refuse to move so others won't have to. She'll suffer the consequences of tough decisions with dignity and face her critics with integrity.

She won't boast or think of herself more highly than she ought. Whether she sits or stands, her work will follow her, not as a footnote on *history.com* or in the margins of someone else's achievement; but rather, she'll demonstrate by her actions that enough is enough. And when a woman says "Enough!" that's when a woman will decide to do what a woman's gotta do.

A decade before civil rights worker Fannie Lou Hamer (another woman who did what she had to do) uttered the words, "I'm sick and tired of being sick and tired," Mrs. Rosa Parks demonstrated such by her actions. She was tired of giving in, she would later write, and on the first day of December 1955, she decided "Enough!"

When a woman's gotta do what a woman's gotta do, she won't quit until her train reaches its destination and her actions will always speak louder than her words. She'll strive to make the right choice because in our lives each of us makes the decision to do or not to do. And once the decision is made life will never be the same for her or for anyone else.

December 1, 1955 was an "Enough is enough" kind of day for Mrs. Parks. When challenged, she stayed in her seat after the White bus driver moved the sign that separated the sections where the two races, both human, could sit on the bus. She refused to move because a woman's gotta do what a woman's gotta do!

The quiet but bold spirit of rebellion within her was certainly inspired, if not fueled, by the roll call of civil rights warriors in the African Methodist Episcopal Church. She also learned from her grandfather and from her study of the Bible that she should stand up for her rights.

As a girl growing up in church, she likely had been taught about the bold actions of AME Church founder Bishop Richard Allen. The formerly enslaved preacher had left the predominantly White Methodist Church because of racist practices that reinforced racial division and hierarchy while preaching about the Christ who had died for all humanity. Moreover, she surely knew that Pastor Denmark Vesey's 1822 rebellion against enslavement in Charleston had been organized with the support of the AME Church. Then, from its inception, the AME publication, *Freedom's Journal*, boldly and actively petitioned legislatures to end enslavement.

Mrs. Parks' faith in God was central to her life and her actions, even those that counted as rebellion. But ultimately, she was all about serving humanity as an expression of her faith. Even after her name was known around the world—whether famously or infamously—for her actions in Montgomery, she continued to serve humbly within her denomination at the church level.

At Saint Matthew AME Church in Detroit, Mrs. Parks served as a stewardess and a deaconess, which is the highest position for a

A Sunday worship service bulletin from St. Matthew AME Church in Detroit with Mrs. Parks' notes from the sermon written inside, 1972 (Photo: Library of Congress, MS014094.MSS85943.0158)

laywoman in the denomination. She also volunteered her secretarial skills in the church office, helping to print the church's weekly bulletins, which she often used to take sermon notes.

Indeed, Mrs. Parks was a woman of great faith and, without a doubt, she prayerfully held onto her seat as she defied the city's desegregation law. Remaining steadfastly positioned after the other Black passengers had complied and as the White bus driver stood over her demanding that she do the same, her faith and her resolve were stretched.

Every person of faith has a few stretching moments in life. Mrs. Parks had many, and throughout her life she proved flexible enough to fit what was needed in the moment. She fit the seat she refused to vacate in 1955. She fit the challenge to move to Detroit when employment opportunities dried up in the South for her and her beloved husband, Raymond. She fit the challenge to continue advocating for civil rights, women's rights, and human rights. She fit the challenge to never compromise her notoriety for personal gain. Instead, she used her renown to strengthen others in the fight for worthy causes. She used her challenges to encourage children to know they can overcome any obstacle to live a blessed life.

Yet no matter how many stretching moments we experience, isn't it marvelous that our faith and our emotions are strong enough to handle our own "Rosa Parks moments"?

Ordinary women and ordinary men accomplish extraordinary things every day. Their achievement didn't grow out of the degradation of enslavement. It grew out of a legacy of courage, guts, grace, dignity, initiative, and resourcefulness.

As a skilled seamstress, Mrs. Parks understood how to put pieces of fabric together to make a garment. Perhaps her early training in sewing also taught her how to fit pieces together until they become whole. She possessed the virtue of patience required to fit pieces together and make the pattern work no matter the size of the client.

Our world needs more people who will sit to take a stand when others have stepped away. For the sake of future generations, we need people who will not shrink in the face of wrong and be steadfast for the cause. Mrs. Rosa Parks was such a person.

The world owes a tremendous debt of gratitude to Mrs. Parks, one we can best pay by following her example and living to serve others. And we are also indebted to Mrs. H. H. Leonards for deciding that now is the time to give us the story behind the glory of the Mother of the Civil Rights Movement and Grandmother of the Women's Rights Movement.

Bishop Vashti Murphy McKenzie
117th Elected and Consecrated Bishop
African Methodist Episcopal Church

## Prologue

I knew Mrs. Rosa Parks in a way that few people ever experience a truly inspirational person. She was far more than an icon of history and a survivor. She was a person whose impact will forever be among us. Mrs. Parks was an "influencer" long before the term became trendy within social media circles.

What she accomplished, she did without malice. All things were done by her with humility and with a kind, loving heart.

I was blessed to share time with Mrs. Parks, her many friends from childhood, and with her co-workers when any of them needed a home-away-from-home for respite.

I use the term "blessed" advisedly, being all too aware that people, myself included, toss the word around so often that it has almost become cliché. But there was nothing cliché about Mrs. Parks. She was outwardly what she was inwardly.

She was who she turned out to be—long before she boarded that Montgomery, Alabama city bus on December 1, 1955.

Suffice it to say this book is about truth and a woman whose faith, honesty, modesty, courage, and immense wisdom moved people—from diverse moral leaders like Nelson Mandela, Deepak Chopra, Malcolm X, and Pope John Paul II, to the smallest of children—to seek and revere her presence.

I believe it is time for the world to celebrate Mrs. Parks beyond the bus—her life, philosophy, and devotion to all people. I am forever grateful to have shared an intimate decade with her.

Mrs. Parks was a humble, straight-forward person. But during her life, she encountered many who either persecuted her or who took advantage or even disregarded who she was—for reasons only known to themselves. Despite this, she was determined to teach love, forgiveness, and compassion at every event and private meeting she attended. She believed this was the only way to rid the world of prejudice. And, of course, whenever she could, she told people of every age, "Get an education. Continue to educate yourself."

Most importantly, Mrs. Parks tried to impart the wisdom of letting go of ego. Only then, she believed, can one accomplish what every person should strive to achieve: love and unity.

By profession, Mrs. Rosa Parks was a seamstress. Her stitching was delicate and precise; she made beautiful clothes. But in the bigger picture, she sewed pieces of people's lives together throughout the world and lifted them up with tenacity, hope, and pure love.

This book weaves the fabric of lessons I learned from her with my recollections of the times we shared. Each thread is spun from her gems of wisdom, which are the soundbites of her life, as I had the privilege of experiencing them.

*Rosa Parks Beyond the Bus* is a collection of memories, anecdotes, incidents, vignettes, aphorisms, and observations, many recorded in a daily journal that I kept. But most dear to my heart are the important lessons I learned while Mother Parks lived with me, when I traveled with her, and when she asked me to sit on the founding board of the Rosa Parks Museum in Montgomery, Alabama. Sister Elaine Steele and Brother Willis Edwards were her other recruits when the museum opened on December 1, 2000.

There was much more to Mrs. Parks than the seat she refused to relinquish on "that" bus. My intent with this book is to call attention to this.

These stories are designed to be inspirational and instructive. The vignettes are random rather than sequential because they reflect the life that Mrs. Parks lived rather than a historical timeline.

She was difficult to define because she was decidedly multi-dimensional. Although many of her peers tried putting her in a box, only wanting her to be known as the woman who refused to give up her seat on the bus, she was more than the estimation of these hangers on. How sad and how wrong this impression of her was—and is.

These are anecdotes of her life that should change that perception.

While in my heart and in my mind, I knew that the moments I shared with her, once revealed, might provide insights otherwise unknown, I have hesitated to put them on paper. The time we spent together was so private and precious. What she discussed with me felt sacred and, therefore, confidential.

The only people who knew she was a regular resident at my home, the O Street Mansion in Washington D.C., were her close friends, business associates, and the lucky people who got to meet her as they visited our museum. So that her privacy was protected, only a few public events were held near Mrs. Parks' rooms. The first few months she was here, we made sure she was not seen by anyone. Understandably, she wanted privacy while she recovered from the assault that had occurred in her Detroit home.

• • • • • •

A little background into the O Street Mansion and the O Street Museum, my residence since 1980, might be helpful here. The O Street Mansion and Museum, as it stands today, is comprised of five interconnected town houses that include over one hundred rooms and eighty secret doors.

Three of the five buildings were designed in 1892 by architect Edward Clark, who was the last architect of the US Capitol at the turn of the 20th century. The building served as his personal home, as well as a few other family members, one of which was Champ Clark, speaker of the house, when Teddy Roosevelt was president.

Originally spanning three row houses, the residence was connected through the basement and main floor and contained separate sleeping quarters for each brother upstairs.

On February 14, 1980, I purchased 2020 O Street, the first row house in the series of connected brownstones, and renovated the townhouse to serve as a bed-and-breakfast and private club. After renovations were completed, I designed and built a new brownstone on an adjacent vacant lot. Later, I was able to acquire three adjacent row houses and incorporate them into a single property.

In 1998, I opened the O Street Museum inside The Mansion. The museum features art, sculpture, music, memorabilia, and written manuscripts and regularly hosts concerts, book-signing talks, film screenings, and tours throughout the year—with a focus not just on the arts, but also on social justice.

Today, the property consists of more than one-hundred rooms of varying architectural, artistic, and design periods, including hand-painted ceilings, authentic Tiffany stained-glass windows, an art deco penthouse, and a two-story log cabin encompassed within this unique venue.

The unique decor and architecture of the building has been cited in many publications, including *Four Blind Mice* (Brown, Little and Company, 2002) by James Patterson, *Afterburn* (Atria Books, 2005) by Zane, and in the young adult series *Gilda Joyce: The Dead Drop* (Dutton Children's Books, 2009), by Jennifer Allison.

At this leg of my journey, people look around at the 110-room mansion, with its thirty-five bathrooms and fourteen kitchens and assume I am wealthy. Far from it.

I started with no money and no business background, no art background, and no design background. Early on, I decided not to pay myself, not to have the museum pay rent, and only have volunteers working for the museum. This ensured that 100 percent of the money we raised through tours and donations went to our arts and social justice programs.

When I turned 65 in 2015, my board of directors advised, "It would help if you told people about the real Mrs. Parks and how you helped her. No one knows this story. Everyone wants to know about her, and nearly nothing of the decade that Mrs. Parks spent here has ever been chronicled. That's not just how you sustain what you have created, but you help bring light to the real Mrs. Parks, and thus help other people to be more like her."

Nearly a decade has passed since that conversation. In that time, we have created several videos about Mrs. Parks' time here, introduced thousands of school children to "Mrs. Parks Treasure Hunts," and created robust programs around social justice and healing through the arts. Annually, an average of 50,000 people come through our doors, where they are exposed to Mrs. Parks and what she accomplished.

We also commissioned Cyril Neville (of the Neville Brothers) to contemporize his classic rap song about Mrs. Parks, titled, "Thank You, Sister Rosa."

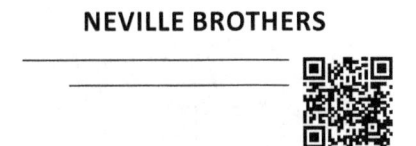

**NEVILLE BROTHERS**

Songwriting legend, ASCAP president, and recovery advocate Paul Williams wrote lyrics to the song "Enough," with Mark Bryan of Hootie & the Blowfish and the Carolina roots group Ranky Tanky composing the music. The seminal line in this brilliant song is, "Hope is a hunger that hate can't control."

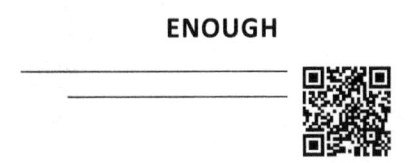

**ENOUGH**

In the 2010s, we were certified as a historic site on the African-American Trail and, with the District of Columbia, are now the driving force behind 51 Steps to Freedom, tracing America's struggle for freedom and equality.

My experience with The Mansion as well as my friendship with Mrs. Parks have affirmed for me in many ways that God does have a plan, and God's way is never easy. And most if not all the time, if you keep things simple and truthful, everything happens the way it should. More than anything, though, Mrs. Parks taught me that we lift everyone up when we share our struggles.

While writing this book, I asked hundreds of people what they knew about Mrs. Parks. Instead of "knowledge," what I heard was, "I love Rosa. She was that lady on the bus, right?" She was who she turned out to be—long before the bus incident in 1955. So now, with the support of R.H. Boyd Publishing, especially Dr. LaDonna Boyd and Rev. Olivia M. Cloud, we have undertaken a sacred mission to let

The United States Postal Service issued a new Rosa Parks commemorative stamp on February 4, 2013, which would have been Mrs. Parks' 100th birthday. (Photo: United States Postal Service via Getty Images)

people know the real Mrs. Parks, as few people did. I am opening up, telling stories that—had Mrs. Parks lived a few more years, with the #MeToo Movement what it is today—I believe she would have told more of her story than is revealed in the four books she wrote.

In her first book, *My Story* (Dial Books, 1992), Mrs. Parks told forthright stories about her mother for the purpose of teaching "beloved children of the world" that they could choose to be what she had become. They didn't need a perfectly manicured childhood and they didn't have to be rich or White to change the world and make a difference. It was a message of hope and a reflection of who she was and always had been.

During our years together, she told me many stories, and I believe that she would want me to share these stories now. Mark Twain wrote a most amazing yet scathing book against war called *The War Prayer*. He ensured it would not be printed until thirteen years after he died.

Similarly, as Mrs. Parks died on October 24, 2005, it is time to recount the stories that she shared with me as well as the experiences we shared. Some are stories that no one else could know. I have written this book in the hopes that current and future generations will come to know Mother Parks in a way that she deserves to be remembered and revered—more profoundly and with insight and understanding.

*Rosa Parks Beyond the Bus* is not just her story. In many ways, the story traces the history of all African-American women who have suffered sexual assault and other untold indignities. These are women who endured discrimination in employment due to race, age, and gender. They managed to survive, and even thrive, despite a system that seemed determined to keep them in poverty and mediocrity. They made a way where there was no road to travel on.

Mrs. Parks is the seminal point in the history of civil, human, and women's rights. Her time is now.

I offer you her truths, as I unfold my thoughts and experiences as her host and traveling companion.

Author H. H. Leonards

*If a movement is to start again
Giving us all the dignity that we deserve—
then it's possible that more leaders of the future will
sit down to stand up for what they believe.*

*It doesn't take money. It doesn't take fame.
That's one of Mrs. Parks' real lessons.*

*H. H. Leonards*

This commemorative plaque marks the spot on Dexter Avenue in Montgomery, where Mrs. Parks boarded the bus for a ride that would change history. (Photo: Katherine Welles/Shutterstock)

# Rosa Parks
# BEYOND THE BUS
## Life, Lessons, and Leadership

H. H. LEONARDS

Top: Mrs. Parks was fingerprinted on February 22, 1956, by Montgomery Lieutenant D.H. Lackey after being indicted as one of the leaders of the Montgomery bus boycott. A grand jury charged one-hundred and thirteen African Americans for organizing the boycott; she was one of seventy three people arrested that day. (Photo Underwood Archives/Getty Images)

Left: Mrs. Parks' official booking photograph (Photo: Universal History Archive/Getty Images)

## Accept Life's Gifts

On December 1, 1955, with one simple act, Mrs. Rosa Parks changed the trajectory of our world. I was a sheltered Midwestern child at the time, living in Lafayette, Indiana, far from the tense racial climate of Montgomery, Alabama. When our paths crossed nearly thirty-nine years later, I had no idea how she had changed the world. After she came to live at The Mansion, she changed my world.

This is how the miracle of Mrs. Parks living here happened.

On August 31, 1994, I received a phone call from a man who introduced himself as Brother Willis Edwards, president of the Beverly Hills Branch of the National Association for the Advancement of Colored People (NAACP). He explained that the NAACP Image Awards were his brainchild, along with Roone Arledge (then chairman of ABC television). Brother Willis (as he liked to be called) later explained that he'd introduced himself to me via his accomplishments so I would know he was "the real deal" and that his request was "a big deal."

He was calling from Detroit, where his "dear friend," Mrs. Rosa Parks, had been attacked in her home. She was in the hospital and could not, would not, return to her house, where the terrible assault and robbery had occurred. She was not a wealthy woman, so the theft and act of violence were quite senseless. Maybe her attacker simply had no idea how truly special she was.

Mr. Willis' wonderfully soft but piercing low tone was captivating. He asked, "Could Mrs. Parks please stay in your hotel until she's healed emotionally and physically?"

The depth of his emotion came through the phone. I could feel his pain. He explained that one of the reasons why he had called me was because he'd heard about our artists and heroes-in-residence program. (We give away approximately one thousand room nights a year, so word-of-mouth does travel.) He also was aware that we had a strict privacy policy. In addition to his request, he wanted to ensure that no one would know she was staying there.

"If I can find her a free flight from Detroit," he proposed, "could she stay there for a few days at no cost?" Mrs. Parks would not be here for long, he advised, as she wanted to return to Detroit after she recovered.

I remember the emotion his words conveyed as if he were saying them to me today. Mrs. Parks wanted to return to Detroit to assure that the children in her neighborhood "would have the chance to become the legends of tomorrow," unlike the young man who had attacked her.

I remember taking a deep, deep breath, trying to figure out what to do, my eyes expanding wider with every breath, and with every word he spoke. As I was exhaling, symbolically letting go of the pain he was describing, he told me how much Mrs. Parks loved children, "all the children in the world who had been left behind." When he finally stopped talking (which seemed interminable), without hesitation, I replied, "Yes, of course. She can stay here at no cost."

A long silence gave us the break we both needed.

In that pause we were reshuffling, figuring out where we were going and what was about to happen. As strange as it may seem, I remember the beautiful classical music that was playing at The Mansion during our silence. I knew intuitively that something very special was about to happen, like when you finally recognize the space between the chords of uplifting music, which transports you and becomes beyond forever, as it takes you to heaven.

I missed the first few words Brother Willis spoke when he finally broke the silence. After I tuned back in, I heard him explain that he would bring Mrs. Parks, accompanied by her very dear friend and fictive daughter, Ms. Elaine Steele.

Ms. Steele and Mrs. Parks co-founded the Rosa and Raymond Parks Institute for Self-Development (RRPI) in honor of Raymond Parks (1903–1977). It is the living legacy of two individuals who committed their lives to civil and human rights. RRPI has operated from both Detroit, Michigan and Washington, D.C.

Under the Institute's umbrella, various programs were developed, like Pathways to Freedom, which was designed to teach young people about the Black freedom movement—from the Underground Railroad to the Civil Rights Movement. Programs within the Institute also taught life skills and community interaction in five-week summer sessions.

RRPI staff and leaders also have helped guided young participants to lend their talents to organizations like the Freedom Writers. RRPI programs have been influential in helping young people to return to school, complete their education, and become involved in their communities.

Brother Willis was also bringing Lois Harris, the trusted assistant of actress Cicely Tyson. (Even today, few people are aware of the close, decades-long friendship between the actress and Mrs. Parks.) Lois would later become Mrs. Parks' caretaker after her stroke at age 92. Lois was a great hidden figure, one of many who were trusted friends in Mrs. Parks' inner circle.

He explained they would need four rooms as well as the room for herself because she would require care around the clock. Rooms were needed for Ms. Steele and Ms. Harris. According to Brother Willis, Mrs. Parks was in terrible shape. He didn't know when she would be released from the hospital, but when she was, she would need a quiet, safe place to rest.

It's embarrassing to admit, but at the time I genuinely did not know the pivotal role Mrs. Parks had played in civil rights history. But I said, "Yes. She should stay with us as long as she wants and needs to."

There are no accidents or coincidences in life. God has a plan for each of us. To each opportunity, we can choose to say, "Thank you, Lord," or we can look the other way and refuse the gifts we are being given. That was something I learned from Mrs. Parks. No matter what happened to her, she always chose to thank the Lord.

Above: Mrs. Parks and Sister Elaine Steele, 1992 (Photo: Library of Congress, 15045, No. 376)

Mrs. Parks and NAACP leader and civil rights activist Brother Willis Edwards, 1998 (Photo: Library of Congress, 15045, no. 121)

## Integrity=Conforming Character to Reality

I must tell you a story that I shared with Mrs. Parks, as it will help to establish the context of this important memory. Hopefully, it will help explain our deep friendship.

I was born and reared in a small Indiana town and personally encountered no Black people until I attended Purdue University. I do not remember meeting or even noticing any African Americans until I worked as a waitress in my college dormitory cafeteria when I was 18, and I remember someone at a table I served asking if he could have a glass of chocolate milk.

"We don't have any. Would you like regular milk?" I replied.

He said, "Yes, in the biggest glass there is." When I brought him a glass, he put his finger in the milk, stirred it, and said, "Now I am drinking chocolate milk."

I told Mrs. Parks that I remember being surprised, not from the laughter of everyone at the table, but because it wasn't until that moment that I noticed everyone I was serving at this table was Black.

I ran back to the beverage station and asked one of my co-workers, "Who is that?" The person seemed stupefied that I didn't know and whispered, "That's Leroy Keyes. He's the star of the football team. The people sitting with him are the only other Black students at Purdue. They are all on the football team."

When I was growing up, my family didn't avoid contact with people who were not White—just the opposite. They brought me up to see beyond race, color, or religion. My mother had adopted a 15-year-old Chinese girl while I was growing up. This was unusual at the time, but I knew better than to question her decision to adopt an older child or, for that matter, one who was Chinese. I was taught not to ask questions of my elders; only to accept what God brings.

To further elaborate on my ignorance in the context of the times, not only were African Americans not living in my hometown, as I explained to Mrs. Parks, our school system had received only a cursory

> **GOING FORWARD**
>
> Every footstep is a triumph over the temptation to stop and go back.

mention of their plight in the context of the Civil War. As I reflect on it now, I find it remarkable that in the more than fifty years since I was in school, teaching an honest and unabridged account of the history of race issues in America is still controversial.

Not only didn't I regard skin color when I served milk to Leroy Keyes, I had never been exposed to the concept of civil rights in high school. It's sad to me now, but nearly twenty-five years after that experience, when Mrs. Parks moved in with me, I was 44 years old and had no knowledge of the infamous Montgomery bus incident nor her relationship to it. Both episodes—my encounters with Keyes when I was his waitress for weeks and not knowing what Mrs. Parks had accomplished until at least three years after she first stayed with me—somehow now seem to have been designed to allow me to meet the heart of the people I had served, rather than to know them as celebrities or icons.

Though later embarrassed by my ignorance, I view my lack of knowledge as a critical component of how things came to be. When I told this story to Mrs. Parks, and later when I apologized for not knowing who she was, she smiled ever so sweetly and patted my hand.

"Lady H," she replied, "this is a great trait. It shows your purity and is the very reason we became such great friends. You know who I really am, not who people make me out to be."

Right: In this letter, Mrs. Parks describes a routine work day at Montgomery Fair department store to illustrate the daily indignities and humiliations Black people in the Jim Crow South endured. The newspapers, city bus lines, stores, libraries, schools, and churches evince segregation as "a complete and solid pattern." The complete letter and other memorabilia are available for viewing at the Library of Congress website, *loc.gov*. (Photo: Rosa Parks Papers, Manuscript Division, Library of Congress, MSS85943, Box 18)

# Montgomery Fair
### COMPANY
22 N. COURT ST. — 29 DEXTER AVE. — 24-32 MONROE ST.

Montgomery 4, Ala.

~~Dear friend~~:

Daily —
Newspapers - black star Edition Colored news separate ~~of y~~. Reason white readers would resent reading the title Miss and Mrs. preceding Colored women's names.

City Bus lines. Front section reserved for white passengers Wash Pk. predominantly Negro, seating space for 10 persons left vacant for white people whether or not they board the bus enroute to town. The bus driver often passes Colored passengers, ~~and~~ with these empty seats, when he thinks enough are standing in the ~~~~ aisle. This means a larger number will be waiting for the next bus.

35

## Love Is All that Matters

In the early evening of late September 1994, Mrs. Parks graced the door of The Mansion, and I began the long journey of wanting to walk in her footsteps to help her attain her goals. The moment we met is etched on my brain. We greeted each other and gently shook hands as she entered.

"Welcome home," I told her, not knowing that this place would become just that to her.

I sigh as I write this because she would never have come to live with me if she had not been assaulted. This horrible, painful episode of her life didn't just change her trajectory, it also irrevocably changed mine. I still feel the pain Mrs. Parks suffered at the hands of someone who, at one point, may have known better, but drug addiction had driven him to choose a life of destruction and despair. I find solace in knowing that Mrs. Parks, rather than cower and hide, chose to work for a greater purpose after the assault happened. She loved living at The O Museum in The Mansion as much as I loved having her here.

Mrs. Parks' cornerstone, her way of life, was constant and consistent. From the time she was a small child to the time she died, she believed that, in everything, to take the long view—always. She believed that one should never compromise for the sake of expediency.

Mrs. Parks arrived in a wheelchair—frail, petite, but beautifully attired. Her hair was perfectly braided and wrapped around her head, as if she were wearing a halo. Mrs. Steele, her best friend, always made sure she was well taken care of. Despite her frail condition, and even though she was physically confined to the wheelchair, I felt her countenance standing tall and resolute when she arrived.

She was very quiet. She also seemed to be in a lot of pain, judging from her body movements and facial expressions. But when she smiled at me as Brother Willis rolled her down the ramp through the red door into what was then known as "The Amnesia Room," she cocked her head to the side and raised her hand to thank me with a gentle handshake; my world changed—immediately and profoundly.

I think about Mrs. Rosa Parks every day. While she passed nearly two decades ago, I cannot help but think about how she would have reacted to the events of the past few years (from voting rights and the murder of George Floyd to the Black Lives Matter movement).

There are so many similarities between what is happening now with what happened during Mrs. Parks' lifetime. We have so much to learn from her. The world knows Mrs. Parks' name. But few have insight into the real woman who did not give up her seat on the bus. Let me give you an example of the real Mrs. Parks, one you probably don't know about.

Did you know that in the early 1930s, Mrs. Parks traveled throughout Alabama for the NAACP, documenting the testimonies of Black women who had been raped? Or that in her first years at the NAACP, she worked specifically on criminal justice in Alabama communities? That meant protecting Black men from false accusations and lynching. It also meant ensuring that Black people who had been sexually victimized and/or assaulted by White people could get their day in court.

Mrs. Parks was a key figure in civil rights, but also in early attempts to rectify sexual injustice for African-American women. This particular issue was one close to Mrs. Parks' heart because in 1931, when she was 17 or 18 years old, a White male neighbor had attempted to assault her. Mrs. Parks successfully fought off the attack and later said of the incident, "I was ready to die. But give my consent? Never. Never. Never."

Sexual assault against Black women was a common occurrence during the first half of the 20th century. In fact, Mrs. Parks had become active in the NAACP many, many years before her fateful commute on "the bus." And she became passionate about documenting rape victim stories because of her own experiences.

In the autumn of 1944, she traveled by herself to Abbeville, Alabama (where her father's family was from) to document the disturbing case chronicled in *The Rape of Recy Taylor*.[1] (Her journal detailing her

## BELIEVING IN YOURSELF TAKES COURAGE

It's all about letting go, taking risks, and opening your heart.

struggles with assault and rape is safely archived at the Library of Congress.)

As difficult as life can be for African Americans today, imagine what it was like for Mrs. Parks living in Alabama during the Jim Crow years. A Black woman could not vote, could not get married to someone White, could not swim in any public pool because someone White may want to swim there, and could not eat or sleep in the same building as Whites. And many Black women and men were not even allowed the dignity of a being called by their name. Let that sink in.

Compound that reality with the hardship of Mrs. Parks growing up during the Great Depression. And she was of African, Native American, and European ancestry. And she was a woman. It is long since the time that these stories of injustice and

Right: Mrs. Parks photographed while engaged in her work as a seamstress not long after the Montgomery bus boycott began, February, 1956. (Photo: Don Cravens/Getty Images)

inequality have been told; because unfortunately there has been little education about social justice and the history of African Americans, it's a story that must be told so that it is not forgotten.

I bring this up here, not just from a historical perspective, but also to shed light on how these events, these facts of life during Mrs. Parks' formative years, affected her personally and how she used the lessons she learned from these events to help lead others. Mrs. Parks firmly believed that hope meant getting a good education, and through education, being proud of your heritage.

By looking at her from this perspective, you can best understand the depth of this truly great woman. Mrs. Parks' life reflected this truth: Your past may not affect your future, but your future always creates your past.

This is a hidden blessing of life.

Right: Mrs. Rosa Parks and H. H. Leonards
(Photo: O Museum at The Mansion)

Bottom: The Mansion on O and O Museum
(Photo: Joy Rahat)

Above: Mrs. Parks (left) with the woman often regarded as the "Queen Mother" of the Civil Rights Movement, activist and grassroots organizer Septima Poinsette Clark (center), and Mrs. Leona McCauley, Mrs. Parks' mother, 1956 (Photo: Library of Congress, 15045, No. 364)

Below: Mrs. Parks (right) and Mrs. Clark at the Highlander School in Tennessee, August 1955 (Photo: Ida Berman, Library of Congress, 15045, No. 1823)

## A Powerful Legacy

Both of us were very shy (that is an understatement). But over time, our bond grew stronger. We talked about what was most important to each of us: God, family—and helping others. Mrs. Parks later told me that she loved me the moment that we shook hands. She said, "You have creator's hands, like me."

As I have mentioned, while our friendship was developing, I still had no idea who she was until one day—about three years later—a guest of our hotel pointed to her sitting in the bay window of our reception room.

"Who is that?" the guest asked.

"Mrs. Rosa Parks," I responded.

It was then that I learned the identity of the woman that the world knew.

I was extremely embarrassed that I hadn't known what she had done in 1955. But then I realized that our Lord had blessed me with not knowing. If I had known, Mrs. Parks would probably not have felt as comfortable as she did here. And she probably would have returned to Detroit, as Brother Willis first said, in just a few days.

Instead, she lived here, in her home-away-from-home, for a decade. In this case, my ignorance turned out to be bliss.

Although Mrs. Rosa Parks is gone now, she is still here, gracing the halls of this peaceful, loving sanctuary. She touched everyone she met. She made everyone around her better. Everyone wanted to be better around her—thus making their contribution to the great circle of life.

What a powerful legacy!

---

**Negro Jailed Here For 'Overlooking' Bus Segregation**

A Montgomery Negro woman was arrested by city police last night for ignoring a bus driver who directed her to sit in the rear of the bus.

The woman, Rosa Parks, 634 Cleveland Ave., was later released under $100 bond.

Bus operator J. F. Blake, 27 N. Lewis St., in notifying police, said a Negro woman sitting in the section reserved for whites refused to move to the Negro section.

When Officers F. B. Day and D. W. Mixon arrived where the bus was halted on Montgomery street, they confirmed the driver's report.

Blake signed the warrant for her arrest under a section of the City Code that gives police powers to bus drivers in the enforcement of segregation aboard buses.

Newspaper article from
*The Montgomery Advertiser*
Friday, December 2, 1955, page 9

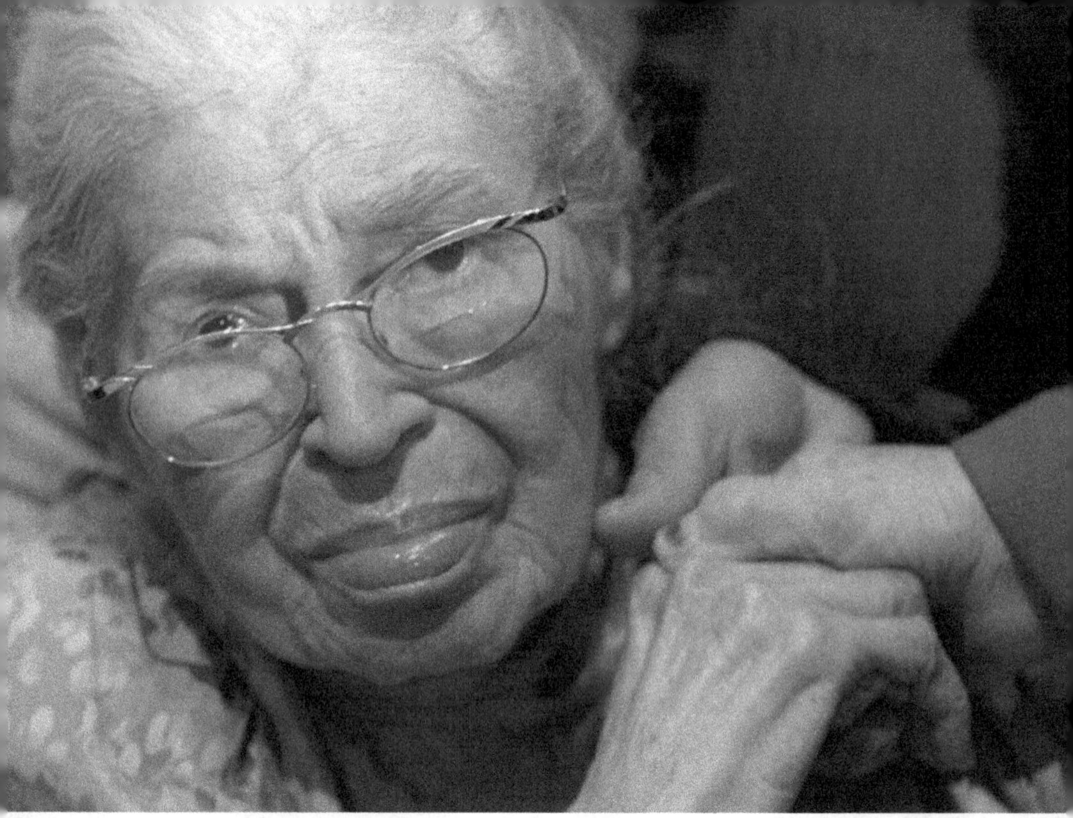

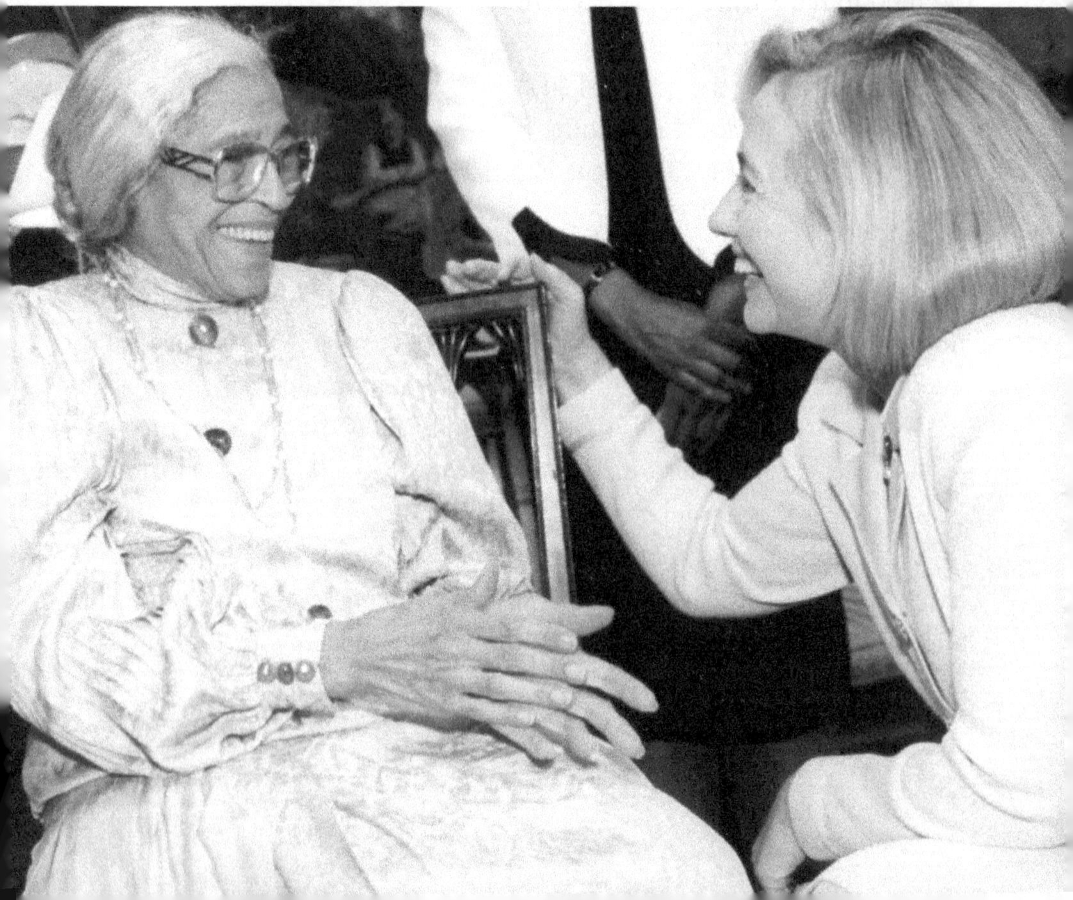

## Authenticity

Throughout this book, I mention Mrs. Parks hands and how extraordinary they were, the power I felt when we held hands and I felt her heart.

The photo taken while Mrs. Parks was the guest of then First Lady Hillary Clinton at the White House shows Mrs. Clinton's joy while talking with Mrs. Parks. The photograph also captures the beauty of Mrs. Parks' hands, how they are the center of the universe—for her, and for all those near them.

Although her hands often hurt severely because of her arthritis, and she felt they always should be covered with gloves, for me they were the most beautiful, most expressive thing about her. Through her hands I felt her power, her focus, and her positive energy, and her love, just by looking at them.

It was as if her hands revealed the poignancy of her story—every indignity and every triumph. Each digit of her hands had been fingerprinted when she was arrested for refusing to comply with Montgomery's segregation laws on a city bus. Her strong hands held up the placard that displayed her inmate number when she was arrested for her participation in the Montgomery bus boycott. Her loving hands had reached out to hug the children she so dearly loved. Her hands reached out to welcome countless celebrities and world leaders into her presence.

Despite all that she endured, or perhaps because of it, Rosa Louise McCauley Parks was the perfect example of authenticity. Her struggle wasn't fabricated or exaggerated to make her a media sensation. She didn't need it to be. Mrs. Parks was a genuine model of strength, beauty, and grace.

Above left: Mrs. Parks holding someone's hand at the Henry Ford Museum in Dearborn, Michigan, during a ceremony commemorating the 46th anniversary of her 1955 arrest (Photo: Jeff Kowalsky/AFP via Getty Images)

Left: Mrs. Parks (left) sharing a light moment with First Lady Hillary Clinton at the White House in the 1990s (Photo: Monica Morgan/Getty Images)

## "Mother Parks"

Although I was an adult when we met, Mrs. Parks quickly became my mentor, my spiritual companion, and my beloved "mother." Early on, I began calling this great woman "Mother Parks," as she had "adopted" me. She became my mentor and a powerful maternal figure to me. She also became a good friend.

I was honored to be one of her many "daughters." She was the perfect example of authenticity. She was a very strong, proud person who chose a life of dignity even though many times, ironically, she faced people and situations that were most decidedly undignified.

I was not the only person who called her Mother Parks. Anyone she became a mentor to—whether male or female, friends, and caretakers alike, addressed her in this manner.

Being called Mother Parks was elevating to Mrs. Parks. Because she had no children of her own, she would beam with such joy when being addressed as mother. And over time—when children from around the world sent her thousands and thousands of letters—she began to understand that all children were her children.

I watched the love affair children had with her. It was real.

The letters she proudly showed me were uplifting, especially when I saw how happy she was to receive them. And she answered every single letter she received. After watching me write in journals on my computer every day, Mrs. Parks began writing a book that addressed many of the letters she received from her international family of children. She said that she needed to do this because the time would come when she could not answer them. She fittingly titled it, *Dear Mrs. Parks: A Dialogue for Youth* (Lee & Low Books, 1996).

Our bond grew closer with time, so much so that she often referred to me as her daughter. The first time she introduced me to someone as her daughter it really surprised me. Every time she did, though, it made me feel both proud and humble. I did not take her use of the word daughter lightly. It meant so much to me. Over time, I came to realize she had become more my mother than the woman who had given birth to me.

Observing Mother Parks in action would affirm for anyone that the amazing construct of the human will. Time after time, it has triumphed against unbelievable odds. But it's not the once-in-a-lifetime dramatic, visible, up-by-the-bootstraps effort that brings enduring success. Rather, it's the day-to-day actions, putting first things first. During her life, Mother Parks encountered many who either persecuted her, took advantage of her, or disregarded who she was for reasons only known to themselves.

## A STORY WITHIN A STORY

News articles about the 1992 attack of Mrs. Parks in her home can be found all over the Internet and in many archival news reports. Most say, inaccurately, that Mrs. Parks had sustained minor bruises and was released immediately. Somehow, key details had escaped those who reported the incident.

In early August 2019, a woman who was touring The Mansion and O Museum told me she was from Detroit and was one of Mrs. Parks' nurses after her attack. She shared with me that Mrs. Parks had been in very bad shape physically, nevertheless, she was kind to everyone and gentle in her treatment of them. I asked if she would participate in a video about her experience while attending to Mrs. Parks. She promptly replied, "Oh, no. I can't. We all signed NDA's (Non-disclosure agreements). I still work there!"

A month later, I was in Detroit. My son Z Stein and I met with Ms. Peek and Ms. Steele to read parts of this book to them. Mrs. Parks had recounted her "assault" to me, but she had never told me anything about NDA's (non-disclosure agreements). And I had never Googled it before to find out that the press never wrote about what actually happened. I told them about the nurse, and asked, "Did the 'truth' escape those who wrote about it?"

"Oh, no," they told me. "Lordy, Lordy, this attack was vicious!" They informed us that Mrs. Parks had a pacemaker inserted in 1988 and the assailant had dislodged it during the attack. Beads of sweat appeared on my forehead. It was hot inside their home, but sweat appeared in response to their recollection of the event. Tears were streaming down my face as I listened to what had really happened.

They told me that Mrs. Parks was worried the attack would reflect unfairly on her neighbors and the good children of Detroit. She was also concerned how "her precious children" would respond. She didn't want them to be frightened, fearing that "bad people would break into their houses."

She still remembered being petrified by the Ku Klux Klan as a child, and how important it had been that her grandmother and grandfather helped her get over these fears.

"Some nights," she quietly recounted, "I vividly recall my grandfather would move a chair to the front of the door, and often slept in that chair, with a rifle in his hands."

It was amazing that she was so badly assaulted but still of the frame of mind to want to protect others.

News article from the *Detroit Free Press*, Wednesday, August 31, 1994, page 1.

## "Mrs. Parksisms"

These are some of my favorite truths that I learned from Mrs. Parks. I don't know where I first saw them, but over the years, I kept them in my notebooks sometimes writing them on scraps of paper.

> *"I have spent over half my life teaching love and brotherhood and feel that it is better to continue to try to teach or live equality and love than it would be to have hatred or prejudice."*

> *"Everyone living together in peace and harmony and love … that is a goal that we seek.*

> *"The more people there are who reach that state of mind, the better we will be."*

Mrs. Rosa Louise McCauley Parks

Mrs. Parks (center) in 1956, riding on a recently integrated city bus following a Supreme Court ruling ending the successful 381-day Montgomery bus boycott. (Photo by Don Cravens/Getty Images)

## To Tell the Truth

I had a lot of fun teasing Mrs. Parks about being on the popular TV show, To Tell the Truth. I have re-watched her segment several times and each time I see it, I love it more. It's a fun slice of history. It also brings home the adage that you can never select who becomes famous. Stuff just happens.

Mrs. Parks very much enjoyed being on this show. She told me that anytime she was asked to tell "her story" she would seize the moment and say, "Yes." She believed that the television shows she was on, the

A still of Mrs. Parks' 1980 appearance on the popular television show, To Tell the Truth, 1980; Mrs. Parks *(right)* and the other two guests were successful in deceiving a few of the panelists. (Image: Library of Congress, webcast-8962)

Rosa Parks Beyond the Bus

movies she was in, as well as the gatherings, meetings, and conferences she attended were never about her. They were simply opportunities to have people hear her story so that her message could be heard on different occasions, to different people.

She told me many times that if people could meet her, perhaps their hearts would change and they would be more open to the concept of human dignity for everyone, no matter their economic, cultural, religious, or racial background. She astutely knew that while the law can change, real progress doesn't occur unless you reach people's hearts. And that's what she set out to do.

To me, that defines a truly great person.

Speaking of truth, Mrs. Parks debunked the myth that she refused to vacate her seat because she was simply too tired to get up after a long day at work.

I was often present when she recounted for others the details of December 1, 1955. Whenever she wrote or when she talked to groups, she would correct the historical inaccuracies about her, saying that history should be accurate.

"I was not tired physically," she would say in her beautifully slow Southern drawl, "or any more tired than I usually was at the end of a working day. I was not old, although some people have an image of me as being old then." When she told her story to others, she would always pause here, for emphasis, as she could watch the surprise in people's eyes. "I was only 42." Mrs. Parks would stop here and take a deep breath. "No, the only tired I was, was tired of giving in."

She told me that as she sat on the bus she remembered the photographs of poor Emmett Till, which haunted her and she could not move.[2] One hundred days after the murder of young Emmett, Mrs. Parks refused to give up her seat on the city bus in Alabama. She said, "I thought about Emmett Till, and I couldn't go back (to the back of the bus)."

The teenage boy being brutally murdered by two White men had weighed heavily on her heart. Later, she became very close friends with Mamie Till-Mobley, Emmett's mother, who visited frequently when Mrs. Parks lived with me at The Mansion.

Mrs. Parks and Mrs. Till-Mobley were tireless civil rights activists and the dearest of friends. Mrs. Till-Mobley always stayed in the Country Room when she visited. They would spend hours talking in the kitchen outside Mrs. Till-Mobley's beautiful white and blue flowered bedroom. The room features a private balcony overlooking the quiet, tree-lined street below. When the weather was nice, the two would sit there. They frequently would tell me they didn't understand how we were in the center of D.C., yet the street below was so quiet.

Another myth associated with Mrs. Parks and December 1, 1955 is that she had taken a seat in the section designated "Whites only." She actually was seated in the first row of the "Negro section" allotted to colored people, Mrs. Parks would explain. However, the city's segregation law stated that once the White section was filled, space could be taken from the seats designated for African Americans. She violated the law by refusing to move from her seat to accommodate a White male passenger who had boarded.

I heard her sigh so many times, sometimes very heavily, as she was forming her words, so what she said was never out of character, and most importantly, never about her. She rarely complained; she would only smile as she endeavored to tell the truth and set the record straight. And yet, no matter how many times she consistently told this story, the press would write that she was an older woman who was simply too tired to get up after a hard day of work and sat in the first seat she could find.

Another myth repeated frequently over the years was a particular anathema to her. Her action on the bus "that day" has been characterized as a "premeditated act of civil disobedience." It was not. Mrs. Parks was adamant about this.

Although she knew that the NAACP was looking for a lead plaintiff to test the constitutionality of Jim Crow laws in the South, she did not set out to be arrested on Cleveland Avenue bus #2857 that day.

Mother Parks told me that she knew the bus driver, and that had she been paying attention to his face rather than fumbling for money in her purse, she would never have gotten on that particular bus. She'd had a previous unpleasant encounter with bus driver, James Blake, and was afraid of him.

In 1943, Mrs. Parks had boarded a bus driven by Blake. She entered the front door of the bus, paid her fare, and proceeded to take a seat. Blake told her to disembark and enter the bus again from the back door, which was a rule imposed by some of the drivers. She got off and decided to wait for the next bus rather than enter through the rear door. She vowed to herself to never ride with Blake again.

According to Mother Parks, James Blake later claimed, "She ruined my life." Several news accounts paint a picture of an embittered Blake, who apparently felt he had been maligned and misrepresented by the media.

When Blake died in 2002, a reporter asked Mrs. Parks to comment. Gracious as ever, she replied, "I'm sure his family will miss him."[3]

She told me one day: *"I had no idea when I refused to give up my seat on that Montgomery bus that my small action would help put an end to the segregation laws in the South. I only knew that I was tired of being pushed around. I was a regular person, just as good as anybody else. There had been a few times in my life when I had been treated by White people like a*

**DID YOU KNOW?**

Did you know that Mrs. Parks still had an outstanding warrant for her arrest—even at her funeral on October 24, 2005? Six months after she died, the Rosa Parks Act was passed in Alabama to allow those who were criminally charged for their involvement in the Montgomery Bus Boycott—including Mrs. Parks—to clear their police records of civil disobedience charges.

regular person, so I knew what that felt like. It was time that other White people started treating me that way."

She also told me that she didn't know how much being in jail had upset her—until she got out. She recalled that her feelings were akin to her reaction when some people came to her house with newspaper photographs of the charred body of Emmett Till.

Despite the many ways her life was impacted because of that day, Mrs. Parks looked back on it and said: *"God has given me the strength to say what is right. Getting arrested was one of the worst days of my life. It was not a happy experience.... I had no idea that history was being made. I was just tired of giving in. Somehow, I felt that what I did was right.... I did not think about the consequences. I knew that I could have been lynched, manhandled, or beaten when the police came. I chose not to move. When I made that decision, I knew that I had the strength of my ancestors with me."*

Below: Mrs. Parks (center) with Mrs. Mamie Till Mobley (left), mother of murdered teen Emmett Till, and Rev. Willie Barrow, possibly at St. John Presbyterian Church in Detroit, 1995 (Photo: Library of Congress, 15045, No. 452)

Right: Exhibit A: Diagram of where Mrs. Parks sat aboard the Cleveland Avenue bus at 6 p.m. on Thursday, December 1, 1955. Photo: Wikimedia Commons, National Archives and Records Administration)

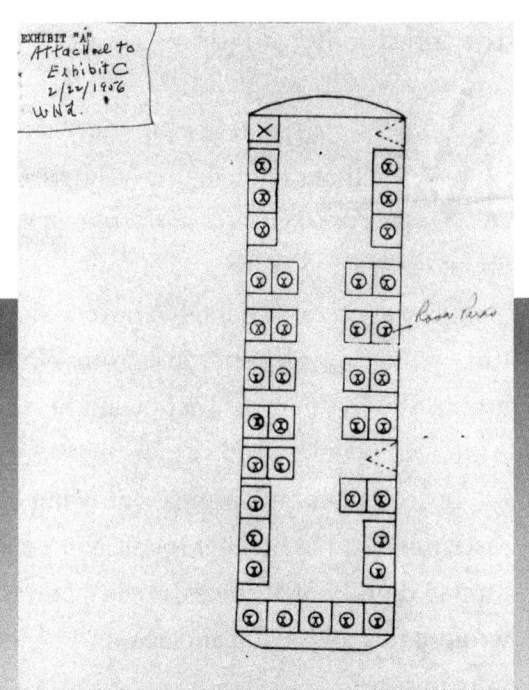

## DID YOU KNOW?

Did you know that riding the bus was how most Black people got to work in 1955? Very few owned a car. Did you also know that women traveling alone or late at night often were fearful of taking the bus?

Mrs. Parks told me she documented many horrific stories for the NAACP about Black women who were raped on the buses in the South. She said many stories were about bus drivers taking women to the end of the bus route. Police officers would be there waiting and would participate in the sexual assault.

Mrs. Parks overcame victimization repeatedly in her life. She helped others with love and compassion. Mrs. Parks also never turned away from situations that others thought might be trouble. She met the devil face-to-face many times.

Mrs. Parks' refusal to give up her seat didn't just spark the Civil Rights Movement, but it also started a Women's Rights Movement that included Black women.

## The Spirituality of Hope

Mrs. Parks didn't see color, although she was not color blind (literally or figuratively). She wrote in her book *Dear Mrs. Parks*: "*Justice and truth do not see color.*" Mrs. Parks was all about justice and truth.

She was proud of her DNA but was deeply affected by discrimination throughout her life—not just from White people but also from other groups she was part of. That meant Black people, White people, Native American people—and yes, women.

Instead of complaining or growing bitter, she chose instead to use discrimination to fuel her focus. Not on just one group, but to fight for human dignity of all races, creeds, and religions. Mrs. Parks believed, wrote, and spoke again and again: "I believe there is only one race—the human race."

I must take a pause here because what I am about to offer was difficult to write. I am a White woman addressing discrimination. Ironically, bias cannot be defined as quickly as it can be felt. Furthermore, it is not clean like the colors of Black and White, so sharp and distinctive on the artist's palette.

I spent countless hours with Mrs. Parks, listening to her, watching her, and hearing stories about her from her inner cadre of colleagues and friends who also stayed with me. She was adamant that associations with people based on any "group" was discriminatory.

She went deeper in her book *Dear Mrs. Parks*, writing:

"*They (the younger generations) must learn from us that love knows no color.*
*They must learn from us that respect knows no color.*
*They must understand that they were all created by the same God, who created us all, in His image.*"

She believed that no progress would be made until no one saw "color," or grouped people by age, or separated them by religion, and stopped judging others by the hierarchy of their employment. She firmly believed that the only way to effect change is to let go of stereotypes and groups and focus on being equal in all respects.

Here's how Mrs. Parks put it into perspective for me. She believed that when you segregate children in school by age (like we have since assembly lines were started), they learn less than in an open classroom of all ages.

Mrs. Parks believed that segregating children by age deprives them of a valuable component of their natural means of self-education. She learned this while a student at Miss White's School because all grades learned together. And it's why her classes at the Rosa and Raymond Parks Pathways to Freedom Institute in Detroit were so powerful. She insisted that children and seniors attend together. She believed that each group taught the other.

Here's another example of what she believed. While she was staying with me, a reporter came to Washington D.C. from California to interview me for a well-known magazine about what it was like to live with Mrs. Parks. She was there at the time, along with Sister Elaine Steele, and Brother Willis Edwards when the reporter arrived. Mr. Willis took the writer—a close friend of his—to her room and then brought her to meet me. But when she met me and saw I am White, she asked to be excused for a moment. When she came back she told me, in front of Mr. Willis, "I cannot interview you for the story because you are White."

Mr. Willis started to laugh and said, "You have got to be kidding me." Then he realized she was not. I could tell he was distraught.

Mrs. Parks was perplexed when she heard the interview had been canceled because I am White. We often joked afterward that if we had money, we should start a magazine called *White Enterprise* and make Mrs. Parks the publisher. Brother Willis would be the editor, just to make a point. "It should be *Enterprise* magazine," Mrs. Parks gently said, "Everyone should be equally represented in the stories and on the masthead."

Mrs. Parks belonged to and supported many groups. She loved the Girl Scouts, the African Methodist Episcopal Church (where she was a deaconess), and the NAACP, to name a few organizations. But she worked to integrate these groups, be inclusive in these groups, and allow people of all ages, religions, and colors to share equally in the joys she felt for being a supporter, of being a member, and of giving of herself to them.

My deep friendship with Mrs. Parks came from our conversations about family and God. And, as important, simply sitting together and saying nothing. We both loved those moments.

Our conversations were about how to honor God, the importance of extended family, her love of children, and how children are the truth of tomorrow. Her focus was on the power of unity, bringing people together.

We did not talk specifically about civil rights, women's rights, or human rights unless our conversations were about how family and God played into these movements. Those conversations came about when we were in meetings with others. And at those meetings, I seldom spoke. Just listened and learned.

One conversation still resonates with me today.

She told me that during the Civil Rights Movement and before sit-ins, prayer was essential. "In fact," she said, "churches were the only place where African Americans could gather legally and feel safe.... Our churches were our lifelines, not only for strength but for accurate news. Throughout the Montgomery Bus Boycott, we began our meetings or sit-in demonstrations with prayer."

Without skipping a beat, she went and read from the book she was working on. Her voice was gentle, but her message seared my soul.

"The important thing to remember is that when people try to hurt us or do mean things to us, God is with us. God gives us the strength to overcome whatever is bad in life, and He gives us the ability to make it better." *(Dear Mrs. Parks: A Dialogue with Today's Youth)*

There are defining moments for each and every one of us. Having Mrs. Parks read this to me was one of my defining moments.

I realized as Mrs. Parks was gently teaching me that no matter what happened to you, it was supposed to occur at that particular moment to teach you, to help you let go of your ego, and think only about others.

You can be quiet, but in your quest, you must believe you can move mountains.

Elaine Steele, Fred Burton, Willis Edwards, and H. H. Leonards posing with artwork of Mrs. Parks created by Gerald Johnson at the O Street Museum in The Mansion. (Photo: O Street Museum in The Mansion)

## "Can Do" and "Yes" Are Magic Words

There was never anything perplexing about Mrs. Parks. You never wondered where you stood with her or what she stood for. Nothing was gray in Mrs. Parks' behavior, words, teachings, and gestures.

Because she was so sure about who she was, you would be assured in her presence of who you were.

Sometimes when you look at famous people, you might wish your life could be theirs. But often, when you get to know the story behind the person, you discover that their life was never easy, often fraught with more pain than imaginable.

What trait, what behavior, propelled them to go on to live meaningful lives, you may ponder. These are the people who picked themselves up by the bootstraps and didn't use their beginnings as an excuse for not living to their greatest potential. Many such persons also firmly believe that their childhood was happier than anyone else's.

Mrs. Parks took her childhood experiences and made them form the greatest childhood ever—by her positive, proactive philosophy.

It wasn't until I began to write this book and reread all the books Mrs. Parks had written—and looked over my own journals from when she was here—that I understood the depth of what she taught me, but also what she had suffered to get to where she was when I met her. Let me explain.

When Mrs. Parks was two, her parents, James and Leona McCauley, separated. Her mother moved the family to Pine Level, Alabama, to live with her parents. Separation and divorce were unusual for the times. Having an additional level of "difference" in her upbringing had a considerable impact on Mrs. Parks. Yet, she said it was "great" because she got to live with her grandparents.

One of her great-great grandfathers was Scottish/Irish and was brought to the United States as an indentured servant. She said that back then indentured servants had no rights and could be treated as badly as slaves, with no repercussions.

Her maternal grandfather, Sylvester, was born enslaved (he was the son of a White plantation owner), but he was not a bitter man (although he was so White, people assumed he was a White man and not an enslaved person). He told her stories about the cruel treatment he endured after his parents died. But he told her the stories to teach lessons, not to embitter her. She told me, "He didn't want his family to be mistreated. His stories made me believe that I must stand up for what is right." She learned courage and strength from her grandfather.

In her autobiography, *My Story*, Mrs. Parks explained that her grandfather had instilled in her the belief that she possessed the capacity to stand for what is right. She learned courage and strength from her grandfather.

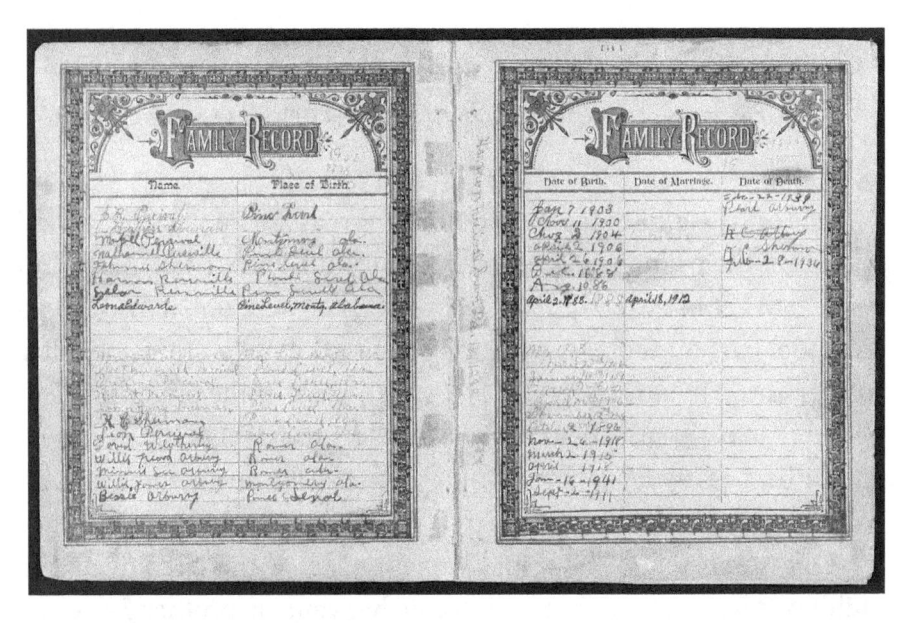

This Bible register (dated ca. 1900) partially charts Rosa's maternal lineage. Accordingly, her great grandfather James Percival, an indentured servant of Scots-Irish descent, married Mary Jane Nobles, an enslaved African. Their daughter Rose married Sylvester Edwards, the son of white planter John Edwards and his enslaved housekeeper and seamstress. They had three daughters: Fannie, Bessie, and Leona Edwards, Rosa's mother. (Photo: Library of Congress, MSS85943, Box OV 17)

Louisa McCauley, Mrs. Parks' paternal grandmother, 1910 (Photo: Library of Congress, 15045, No. 2336)

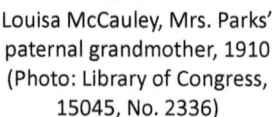

Anderson McCauley, Mrs. Parks' paternal grandfather, photographed ca. 1900 (Photo: Library of Congress, 15045, No. 1319)

The only work her mother could get was as a schoolteacher a long way from their home. Such jobs were difficult for African-American women to get in the early 1900s. Boys of color were not allowed to go to school past third grade, and girls of color did not go to school after fifth grade. Why no schooling? Depriving them of the opportunity to get other jobs because they could not read and write ensured that there would be a ready labor force in the cotton fields or in some similar form of work.

One thing that always struck me as Mrs. Parks recounted her childhood was that she always protected her younger brother, Sylvester. She told me that her grandmother, Rose, reminded her about a time when she was about to give grandson Sylvester "a whooping" with a little switch. Mrs. Parks recalled, "I said, 'Grandma, don't whip Brother. He's just a little baby and doesn't have no mama and no papa either.'"

Sylvester J. McCauley, Mrs. Parks' brother, during WWII, 1942 (Photo: Library of Congress, 15045, No. 1366)

I gathered from this story that Mrs. Parks, at a very young age, became committed to helping those who could not help themselves. Grandmother Rose would later tell her that she was so taken aback she put the switch down and decided she would not whip him—at least not that day. Mrs. Parks had an additional perspective. She said, "The habit of protecting my little brother helped me learn to protect myself."

Rather than be a domestic servant, their mother chose to set a higher standard for her children and teach. But to do so, she had to live in another community far from her children.

Mrs. Parks understood her mother wanted what was best for her children. "She would try to come home on the weekends when she could." But it wasn't easy for anyone—not for young Rosa nor brother, nor for the many "relatives" who passed her around when she went to Montgomery to get an education as a young child. And certainly, not for her mother.

Mrs. Parks was very proud that her mother was a teacher. In her biography, she explained that her mother taught her not to judge people by their possessions, a sentiment at which I still marvel.

She learned from other people. She was mentored by other people than her family too. She learned from her mentors not to seek the limelight. She became a woman of great faith. She understood the spirituality of humility. But through her family she learned that first, she had to be proud of herself and her people, all of them.

As much as she admired her mother, though she felt her absence, Mrs. Parks was also happy that her maternal grandparents had reared her. Without the lessons they taught her, she would never have become Mrs. Rosa Parks. Their deep but strict love, discipline, and guidance helped to shape her character.

She said so many times, "If I can save one life, I have done something worthwhile."

## Life Is a Jigsaw Puzzle: Eventually, Everything Fits

Because public education for African Americans in the South often ended after the third grade for boys and the fifth for girls, Mrs. Parks was enrolled by her mother in a private school for the sixth grade. Her mother sent her to Montgomery to attend Miss White's School for Girls on what she was told was a scholarship, which to her was very prestigious. It wasn't until much later that she learned that her "scholarship" meant she was expected to clean the bathrooms and keep the school clean.

She did this with joy, never resentment. Mrs. Parks felt it was essential to candidly tell stories about her personal life. She felt that if she was honest about her struggles, children of the world would know they could come from any background and any hardship and be the person they wanted to be. Life is about making positive choices.

Did you know that when little Rosa went to school in Montgomery (at age 11), that Black people were not allowed to get inside buses, only ride on the tops of them, where luggage was stored?

The school's vocational and academic curriculum was strict: school uniforms were mandatory, while jewelry, cosmetics (and hair straighteners) were discouraged. Daily devotional services also included lectures on racial equality. The lessons she learned carried her throughout her lifetime. And later, she used this school as a model to create her own school in Detroit, the Rosa and Raymond Parks Institute for Self-Development (RRPI).

Mrs. Parks also learned how to become a seamstress at Miss White's school. She loved creating new things and she loved teaching others how to sew. The school was dedicated to teaching young ladies about home economics (back then, it was called "domestic science"). It was a trade school, so all the girls who attended would have a marketable skill through which to earn a livelihood. She often spoke about how thankful she was having attended the school because it allowed her to escape toiling in the fields, the employment fate of most African Americans in the South.

Because all the teachers were White, Mrs. Parks had the opportunity to meet and learn from White people as she had never encountered them before. Prior to the school, she had only engaged White people in the manner expected in the South during those days. She later credited Miss White's School with teaching her that she was a person of dignity and self-respect. She also learned not to regard herself as having lesser value because of her skin color.

"With knowledge, we gain confidence. There is no future without an education," she wrote in *Dear Mrs. Parks*.

This is another reason why she started her institute and her Pathways to Freedom programs. She said, "I want all children to have a good family life. And that doesn't mean it has to be at home."

## Building a Loving Community

While in school in Montgomery, Mrs. Parks was sent to live with many different "relatives." I eventually learned that they weren't necessarily relatives, although at the time, she was told they were. This was another reason she felt like an orphan.

Enslaved families often didn't know where their blood relatives were because all or some members of a family could be sold at the hand of the slave owner. Family members could be scattered anywhere within the slaveholding states. This resulted in a communal culture where everyone helped everyone else as if they were family. Many African Americans created what sociologists call "fictive relationships."

I heard Mrs. Parks speak to children on numerous occasions, and she would always tell them about enslavement and its aftereffects on Black people. "At the time, if you tried to bond with people, they would separate you, so we strived to be one community. This is when one family had food, everyone in the community shared it. We all came together to help each other."

Mrs. Parks had a gift for building a loving community all around her. She took the extra step to make loving communities possible.

One thing she never did—from the time she was a little girl to when she had a severe stroke the last year of her life—was complain.

No matter what happened to her, she always kept a cheerful disposition. She believed, "When you are smiling and eating food, even if it doesn't taste great, or if you aren't full, as there isn't enough food, it all tastes better when you are smiling."

She often added, "And praying, with your extended family."

## Memories of Her Mother

No matter what happened to Mrs. Parks throughout her lifetime, she made each experience a positive part of whom she wanted to become.

Mrs. Parks said she felt like an orphan when she was a girl, as her mother worked away from home to provide for their family after her father left them. She forthrightly documented this in her autobiography: "My mother was around 25 years old by the time I was born, but she always said she was unprepared to be a mother."

She also explained in *My Story* that her own mother had spent a lot of time crying, weeping, distressing about what she was going to do and how she would take care of a child.

Expressing these realities was important to Mrs. Parks. She didn't share these experiences in order to discredit her mother; but rather, she loved her deeply and understood where her honesty was coming from. She also empathized with her mother.

Mrs. Parks felt it was essential to candidly tell stories about her personal life. She felt that if she was honest about her struggles, children around the world would know they can come from any background and any hardship and be the person they wanted. "Life is about making positive choices," she frequently told me.

Raymond Parks (second, left) with three men in front of Atlas Barber & Beauty in Montgomery, Alabama where he worked as a barber, 1933 (Photo: Library of Congress, 15048, pg. 11)

"I want people to know my truth," she said often. "This is important. Children can have adversity in their lives, but it doesn't have to affect who they want to become."

She wanted children to know that what happens to them as a child is not what's most important. But rather, it's how they choose to react to what happened. By telling her story, she felt children could better understand that no one's life is perfect.

Still, if you asked her what her childhood was like, she would always respond, "perfect!" And that is what she truly believed.

It was so important to Mrs. Parks to honor her mother's sacrifices. She understood that the key to self-betterment was a good education because she had seen these sacrifices. She also was grateful for what her mother had done for her, given the reality of life in the early 1900s. If it wasn't for her mother's determination to send her daughter to live with others when she was old enough to attend a private school, she knew she might have become a faceless woman toiling in cotton fields only to earn poverty wages. She knew firsthand what getting a good education would mean to her future.

When Mrs. Parks married her beloved husband, Raymond, her mother moved in with them. Her husband, "Parks" (as Mrs. Parks always referred to him) was very happy to have her with them. His mother and grandmother had died, not long before they married, and he loved having family around him.

This foundational way of life—taking care of your family, and your extended family, as well as your community—was one of the reasons Mrs. Parks loved, honored, and respected her husband as deeply as she did. He loved having her mother live with them. And he took care of her as lovingly as he had his own mother and grandmother.

She knew that the world was complex but broke it down into simple goals. She understood—and honored—her mother. She knew she would not have become the woman she did had it not been for her mother or her experiences growing up.

## There Are Many Ways to Climb a Mountain

I have had many sleepless nights and migraine-filled days, praying and writing in my journals about my hesitancy to tell the story about the horrific times Mrs. Parks was confronted with—the inhumanity of humankind and the ugliness of the hatred expressed through physical assault.

Few people, even those in her personal circle, knew that Mrs. Parks studied the tenets of various religions, including Judaism, Hinduism, Buddhism, and Catholicism. The teachings she learned from her studies were the subject of many discussions she and I had in our private moments.

Mrs. Parks taught me that from 1910 to 1940, more than two thousand primary and secondary schools and twenty Black colleges (including Howard, Dillard, and Fisk universities) were established in whole or in part by contributions from Jewish philanthropist, Julius Rosenwald. At the height of what she called "Rosenwald Schools," nearly 40 percent of Black people in the South were educated at one of these institutions.

Julius Rosenwald endowed Tuskegee and sat on its board. He was a friend of Booker T. Washington.

Other than her own faith, Judaism was the first religion Mrs. Parks encountered. She started learning about Judaism after she met Rosenwald while she was a student at Miss White's School, which he had funded. He was the president of Sears & Roebuck at the time, and when he told the students there that Alvin Roebuck was African American, it was as if he seemed to "walk on water."

When she learned that the NAACP, the Leadership Conference on Civil and Human Rights, the Southern Christian Leadership Conference (SCLC), and the Student Non-violent Coordinating Committee (SNCC) were funded and staffed primarily by Jewish volunteers, she started learning about Judaism in earnest.[4]

She learned that Judaism teaches respect for the fundamental rights of others as each person's duty to God. "What is hateful to you, do not do to your neighbor" (*Babylonian Talmud*, Shabbat 31a).

I keep going back to a conversation we had about how she learned from her Jewish friends during the early days of the Civil Rights Movement, about a concept they called "*Takun Olam*."

I did not know what *Takun Olam* meant. She explained *Takun Olam* teaches that to repair the universe, you must be honest—a basic principle that guided Mrs. Parks' life.

She and I often discussed that we all bear the responsibility for our personal moral, spiritual, and material welfare—and the welfare of society at large. This is the true meaning of social justice: repair the world with love.

What is more horrifying than physical rape? How do you repair the universe after that? *Takun Olam*.

Love is all that matters.

## It's All Good

I don't know how deeply Mrs. Parks suffered as a young child after her father left. Mrs. Parks told me an adage that she believed in: "Before you judge a man, walk a mile in his moccasins."

I could read psychology books that provide insight into how she might have been affected. But honestly, I don't know if she compartmentalized her experiences, or if she simply let them go. When I was with her, there were indications of what she must have suffered, but if you are not the person living the story, you can never be sure.

Child psychologists say that children who are "abandoned" by a parent often are afraid to form attachments in later life. Mrs. Parks had a loving grandfather and grandmother who were always there for her. Because she felt their love, she was able to give her unconditional love to her brother, Sylvester. She defied odds.

She told me that as a child, she believed that no matter what happens, it's all good. She believed strongly that there was a reason for everything. She always seemed to have understood that it's not what happens to you, and it's not what you do. It's how you grow through it.

Whatever happened to her, she stood up firmer in the belief that the Lord had a plan for her, that every breath was "glorious."

Child psychologists also might tell you that daughters whose mothers don't spend a lot of time with them are afraid of motherhood and of becoming attached to others. While she had no biological children, Mrs. Parks became the mother of the Civil Rights Movement. She should be recognized as the grandmother of the Women's Movement. She devoted her life working with children. She also had long-term relationships with her husband, brother, and several friends. She consistently focused on her mission, visions, and values. Mrs. Parks defied norms.

She was open and wrote about her mother's frailties—not with anger, but with unabashed, unconditional love. She talked openly about how difficult it was after she became famous and an encounter with her father when he tried to come back into her life decades after he had left. She agreed to see him for the sake of her brother. Unfortunately, he didn't seem interested in her brother, making the reunion even more painful for her.

Through her life experiences, she wanted to children understand that love and compassion are the cure; there is no place for anger. She hoped that her story would help children know that, like her, they can rise, with love in their hearts. Mother Parks was proactive in everything. A trailblazer in so many endeavors. Her fortitude was never about her skills; it was about her will, which she always put in God's hands.

By any account, Mrs. Parks did not have an easy childhood. Young Rosa had to drop in and out of school to take care of her ailing grandparents. Then, her mother became ill, as did her brother. She had to work in the fields barefoot to help support her family. Then, as if that weren't enough, there was the ever-present menace of the Ku Klux Klan, never allowing them to feel safe or secure.

Despite all she endured, she lovingly reflected upon her childhood and recalled that it was the happiest time of her life, especially when she got to go fishing. Even as an adult, she loved to go fishing.

She also loved who she was and her heritage. She was proud of being White, Black, and Native American. She was open about her DNA long before anyone spoke of their diverse racial composition. She wrote about her family and its history in her own books. She was a regal, strong willed, grand lady who rose up from the hatred, ignorance, and poverty of the Deep South to change the world.

In my imagination, in my lexicon of how you rise above the challenges that happen in your life, the life of Mrs. Rosa Parks points to why her faith was so important to her (and to me). Her life story also reveals why leading an exemplary life was so significant to her success.

Right: Mrs. Parks' father, James McCauley, 1923. Courtesy of The Rosa and Raymond Parks Institute (Photo: Library of Congress, 15045, No. 371)

Below: Mrs. Parks childhood home in Alabama, 1916 (Photo: Library of Congress, 2019630507)

## The Little Yellow School Bus

I used to own a little yellow school bus. It was my only vehicle. I would drive Mrs. Parks in the bus when she had important meetings in D.C. She always sat in the front seat, close to me.

The irony was not lost on us. Imagine Mrs. Parks, Elaine Steele, and Brother Willis Edwards—with a White woman driving—pulling up to places like the White House, as we sometimes did, in a little yellow school bus! Mrs. Parks was allowed to stay on the bus, but for security purposes, everyone else had to get off to pass security. With Mrs. Parks on board, we were always allowed to drive right to the front door after we were "checked out."

Mrs. Parks was treated with respect and understanding when we visited presidents Bill Clinton and George H. W. Bush in that little yellow school bus. The Secret Service told us very few people were allowed the privilege of driving to the front steps of the White House.

I would drive her to church every Sunday in that bus. I would also pick her up at the airport when she returned from one of the many events where she spoke. What was great about the school bus is that when I got to the airport, I could just park out front (at that time there were bus stops in front of Reagan National Airport) and go right to the gate to get her.

What a bonus! We could leave the bus anywhere and not get a ticket. I could even drive in the bus lanes in New York City. No traffic cop or parking meter monitor would ticket a yellow bus that said on its side, "School Bus." The only person who didn't like the bus was my young son, Z. When I drove him to school, he would have me park at least a block away so no one knew he was arriving on his mother's bus.

Mrs. Parks always donned a huge child-like grin as we chugged along through the streets of Washington D.C. in the little yellow bus. It was great fun!

I sold the bus right after September 11, 2001. That morning, The Mansion was hosting a major three-day conference for senior staff

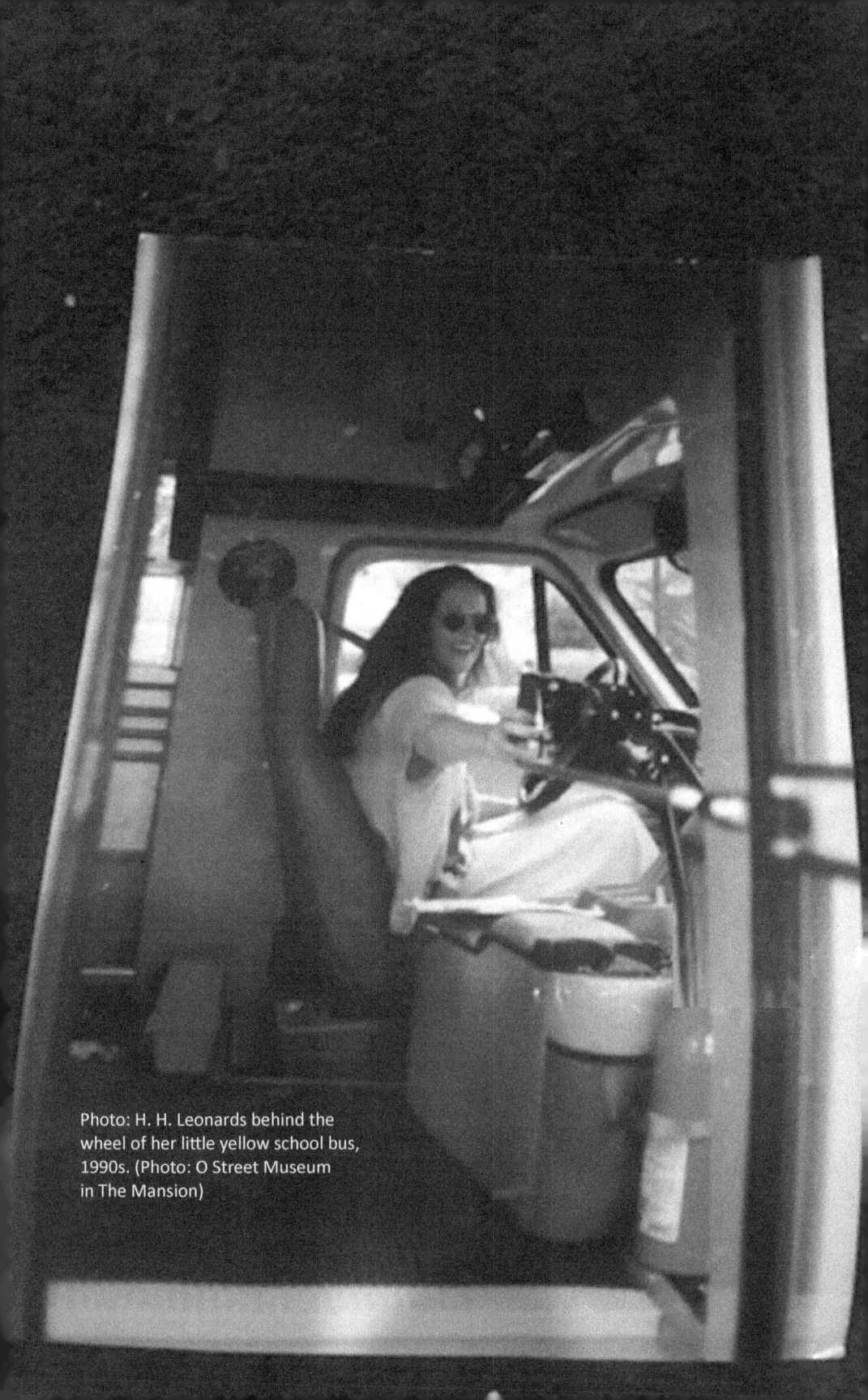

Photo: H. H. Leonards behind the wheel of her little yellow school bus, 1990s. (Photo: O Street Museum in The Mansion)

representing an international bank. I went into the meeting room (which I seldom did) and gave a note to the woman in charge that informed the group that the World Trade Center in New York City had just fallen. Remember, at the time no one knew what had happened, except that two jets had crashed into the Twin Towers.

She came out fifteen minutes later and said, "Please do not bother us again. We are used to terrible things happening all over the world. We are here to discuss important issues that go beyond one incident. We need to continue."

I learned an important lesson that day. Whatever happens, even if we think that it is the worst possible situation, for someone else, it may not be. There is always something that someone else considers worse.

Later that afternoon, I was told that the wife of a gentlemen in the meeting was in one of the buildings. Even he did not come running out to see what had happened. Fortunately, she was one of the lucky ones that escaped.

The next day, my staff and I made sandwiches for those working at the Red Cross building who were providing aid to the survivors of the Pentagon crash. I drove the yellow school bus loaded with sandwiches to the building, and then got back in the bus and drove, by myself, to Gettysburg.

I spent a few hours in the fields of graves there, gathering strength. Then I drove to where my son was, in school near Newburyport, Massachusetts. I wanted him to see me, to know I was okay after what had happened. That he would be okay.

It was a long, bumpy, and sad drive for me. Because I didn't want to have to drive home alone, I sold the bus on the spot to my son's school.

When I told this story to Mrs. Parks, she simply nodded her head, smiled, and said, "I am so glad his school got my bus." We never spoke again about our little yellow bus.

I was glad then that I had sold the bus, but in retrospect, I wish I hadn't because of all the memories of Mrs. Parks in the front seat of the bus, smiling. She was so happy riding around in it.

## The Assault: What Really Happened

Mrs. Parks' most historic hour happened on "the bus," December 1, 1955, but perhaps the moment that revealed the depth of her strength occurred nearly forty years later when Joseph Skipper broke into her home.

When she was 81 years old, Mrs. Parks was robbed and assaulted by a Black man in her Detroit home on August 30, 1994.

The press wrote that she was released from the hospital with minor injuries. I found only two public comments about the assault online:[5]

*"I tried to defend myself and grabbed his shirt," she explained.*

*"Even at 81 years of age, I felt it was my right to defend myself."*

In truth, Mrs. Parks was beaten so badly (in her words "assaulted") that her pacemaker was dislodged. It was only later that I learned she also had been sexually assaulted during the attack.

She testified against her assailant in court because, as she explained, "I had to…for all the women who had ever been assaulted and their stories were never told."

Found guilty, Skipper was given a sentence of eight to fifteen years in prison. But before he was even arrested for the crime, her assailant was dealt a bit of street justice from community ruffians after they had gotten word of the crime.

She once told me, during one of our afternoon chats that she pressed charges because "You can't abuse women without there being any consequences."

While Mrs. Parks really believed in there being consequences to actions, she was a Christian. She forgave her assailant, but she didn't forget what he had done to her.

These steps and this focus were important to her. It was remarkable to witness the way she processed what happened in her life, good or bad.

She said that each incident had made her, in the long run, more resolute to help other people. Her focus never wavered. She was able to pick herself up and move on because of this uncomplicated way of looking at how to bring meaning to your life: "When I die, I want to be stronger than when I started."

She knew that it would be tragic to get old and then compromise what she lived her life for. I believe this is why, when she healed her spirit and body, she also became stronger and more resolute.

Disciples never die.

The Russian Tea Room and circular closet door. (Photo: O Street Museum in The Mansion)

## Mrs. Parks' "Room"

Mrs. Parks told me that she felt safe and comfortable at The Mansion. She mostly stayed here with her best friend, Mrs. Elaine Steele, as well as with Brother Edwards, who was the greatest advance man ever.

When I bought 2018 O Street NW (known as The Mansion), although it had originally been connected, the entrances between the homes had been blocked as it had undergone several transformations. The original owners, the Clarke family, separated the three homes, then moved out because it was too stressful living connected to a "ne'er-do-well" brother. In the 1930s two of the three homes were converted to a "rooming house" for FBI agents. It became housing for students during the protest movement of the sixties. Finally, it was converted back to a single-family residence.

Mrs. Parks suite was located in the 2018 O Street NW section.

When I bought it the property, the "bones" were there, but it was neglected and ugly. I am sure it had been a beautiful house at one time, but by the time of my purchase, it had lost all its character. Except, when we did the demolition, we found an original Tiffany window behind a plaster wall. The window itself was so badly damaged that it could not be repaired, but the transom was in good condition. After extensive reconstruction, it was placed in what is now called "The Russian Tea Room," over a circular closet that we added. This room was right under Mrs. Parks' bedroom and was always the first room she entered off the elevator on the second floor.

She loved this room.

For Mrs. Parks' room, I had been given a bed from which I got the inspiration for the design of her room. In pictures that we took during the renovation, the "highlight" was a slime green bathtub that we replaced with a mahogany wooden tub.

I talk a lot about the sequence of life and that things are supposed to happen in the order that they do. Mrs. Parks' room was completed a week before she arrived. She was the first person to stay in the room after it was created. I named it in her honor. Today, it is exactly as it was when she was there.

Mrs. Parks gave us many items during her stay. They are spread around The Mansion and O Museum, as well as in The Rosa Parks Safehouse, across the street (more of that later). She gave us signed art by her friend, Artis Lane, who stayed with us frequently, as well as copies of the books that she wrote, and cookie jars—she loved cookies and was a great baker.

The one book she told me she wanted to write, but hadn't, was a healthy lifestyle cookbook. A dream of hers was to help children eat properly. Today, if you visit the exhibit devoted to her at the Library of Congress, you will find some of her healthy recipes. Someday, someone will help fulfill Mrs. Parks' dream and create her cookbook.

She also gave us things that today some would describe as racist because they are "picaninny" pieces. But she loved them, as much as she loved eating Uncle Ben's® rice and Aunt Jemima® pancake mix. She was proud to buy products that depicted African Americans on the label.

Among the items in her Library of Congress collection is her "featherlite pancakes" recipe, written by her own hand on the back of an envelope. Mrs. Parks always recycled anything she could. She never threw out what she could reuse.

Faith, honesty, modesty, and courage were the four foundations of Mrs. Parks' life. For her, life was never about what you own since you can't take it with you when you pass through the pearly gates.

Mrs. Rosa Parks' bedroom at The Mansion (Photo: PBJ Pictures, O Museum in The Mansion)

Rosa Parks Beyond the Bus

## Coming Back Stronger

Mrs. Parks often talked about being thankful for every day she was alive. It didn't matter that she had difficulty getting out of bed in the morning or if it started raining when she had no umbrella. She was simply happy to be able to help others.

Mrs. Parks told me that although "the incident" that brought her to The Mansion was bad, the effects were compounded because it brought back memories she had of other assaults—both verbal and physical—she had endured from childhood and beyond.

While she rarely talked about it publicly, she frequently told me how difficult it was growing up in the South. It was painful for me to hear this graceful, beloved woman tell such horrific stories. She didn't tell me to elicit sympathy, but rather to simply tell her story and, as she said, the story of most Black women.

What was most remarkable to me was observing Mrs. Parks consciously choosing to rise above the situation. Each time something bad happened, she chose to live the rest of her life with even more purpose.

Remarkably, when something painful happened to Mrs. Parks, she chose to use the experience to make herself stronger and more resolute. With each painful event that she suffered—attempted rape, lynching of friends, houses burned down, verbal and physical assaults, Emmett Till's death (which had a big effect on her) and the death of her husband, brother, and mother in quick succession—she responded by choosing to lead her life with even more purpose.

She recounted that she believed the incident that brought her to me happened so she could have a deeper understanding of her beloved brother, Sylvester's PTSD, suffered as a result of his experiences during World War II. She said that she wished she had known then what she knew at the time. Had she understood the horrors of what he was reliving, she believed she would have been able to help him and his family more.

After she moved to The Mansion, when she became stronger, physically, and spiritually, she began meeting with PTSD groups with a passion. She said the attack made her resolve to help soldiers like her brother heal, and that was part of her healing. By talking to them, she was healing herself.

I am proud that from the early days of the O Museum, we have had a robust Heroes in Residence program. Through the program we offer lodging to individuals who need respite—a place of spiritual, emotional, and even physical healing. Through our Artists in Residence programs, we strive to empower people to do what they love—dare to be different—and have fun. The Artist in Residence program is designed to inspire creativity, diversity, and imagination through the fusion of the arts, science, and sports. Each year, we give more than one thousand room nights to our heroes and artists in residence.

Our first heroes were those returning from combat. When these heroes stayed here during Mrs. Parks' residency, she would spend extra time talking with them privately. She said this was one of the reasons she loved being here.

But know that she didn't bounce back from her traumas right away. She took time to heal spiritually, emotionally, and physically, using this time to replenish her soul. Sometimes it took her a few months (depending on what happened) and sometimes as many as two years. When she came back, she returned as a fierce, focused, loving tiger. She told me that taking time to heal was critical to being able to help others. First you needed to heal yourself because you cannot give to others without having done that.

Mrs. Parks believed strongly that everyone can make a difference, and that you must not be afraid to take the first step on your journey to help others. She was always so delighted by what a new day brought.

At her 83rd birthday party, celebrated at The Mansion, she said, "I have come to realize there is always more in life to learn. The key is to learn different ways to reach out and help others, with empathy, compassion, and love." She also believed that helping others first was the path to helping yourself.

What also drove her was how strongly she believed in forgiveness—and the importance of hope. Whether it was teaching these concepts at her institute in Detroit, supporting a food bank, traveling to meet with children throughout the world, taking bus tours with children to help them learn about their history, bringing Angela Davis to Detroit for a rally, testifying against Judge Clarence Thomas, or simply writing thousands of letters to those who wrote to her, she dedicated her life to others.

Fame does not shield anyone from what "life" brings. Mrs. Parks took her suffering and hardship and used them to grow—both inwardly and outwardly.

## The Art of Wielding Influence

Mother Parks repeated her lessons, her message, many times, in different words and actions. "It's simple" she often said, "When you fall down, you get up."

She also taught frequently, "Whatever you do, think positively and be concerned about other people."

She also continually taught what the Bible teaches: to look at everything in terms of not succumbing to that which will destroy your physical health and mental health.

Mother Parks led an exemplary life because she wanted nothing to get in the way of her message. She taught by using herself as the example, not just in the classroom, but also when she spoke publicly. It was her message even when accepting an honorary degree or accepting an honor, "When you fall down, you get up."

"Whatever you do, think positively and be concerned about other people" was her message when she was named one of the 100 most influential people of the 20th century by *Time* magazine, along with

Mother Theresa, Princess Diana, Raisa Gorbachev, Albert Schweitzer, and Elie Wiesel.

But here is where Rosa Parks' life gets interesting and why she defied the odds. Everyone loved her, everyone revered her, but not a lot of people knew that she was a proud, active member of the Black Panther Party. One of her favorite personal moments was having the opportunity to talk at length with Malcolm X. While many others who were members were followed by the FBI and persecuted by the press, Mrs. Parks was not.

Not many people know that she did not believe in what Dr. King believed in, which was non-violence. Although, she went on the record to say that without Dr. King's non-violence movement, she doubted that the Civil Rights Act would have passed without Dr. King's guidance and insistence in non-violence.

She recalled having guns in her home when she was a toddler. She believed her grandfather sitting at the front door night after night with a rifle in his arm had kept their family alive.

She believed in the Bible's words (Exodus 21:24; Leviticus 24:19–20) "An eye for an eye…." But she also held within her heart the compassion that Jesus taught during His Sermon on the Mount (Matthew 5:38-42).

Mrs. Parks actively campaigned for Black political candidates, not just in Detroit, but also across the country. She took part in a variety of groups, mobilizations, and protests. She was active in challenging U.S. involvement in Vietnam (through which she became a friend of Muhammad Ali) and spoke frequently against police brutality. During the Detroit riots in 1967, her husband's barbershop was destroyed; not by the rioters, but rather, by the police.

Was she a radical?

The answer is in your heart. That's what she would say if you asked her this question. And know that whatever you think her answer would be, she would be smiling at you and holding your hand. "Think what you want to think," she would say. "The important thing is to ask the question. To ask any question you want. For only by asking questions, can you learn."

So, how did Mrs. Parks come out unscathed by the FBI and so beloved and respected by the press, while being such an activist? Perhaps it's because she did so quietly, with no fanfare. She wasn't there to promote herself, just the cause. Perhaps it's because she understood the power of leading an exemplary life, being authentic, and being true to herself.

As a result, people listened to her words and her stories. They listened and remembered because she listened to them. People described Mrs. Parks as being "quiet." Quite the contrary. Yes, she listened more than she talked. But when she did talk, because she had listened first, she gave great guidance and provided historical perspective. "Live every breath" was her abiding message.

Mrs. Parks took the long view of things, never the short gain. She wrote and spoke about this often, and discussed these things with her close friends, who then, like me, spread out to tell her message.

While I am paraphrasing, this is what she preached: "Make a decision, not because it will be popular, but because it is the right thing to do."

Filmmaker Spike Lee said, "Do the right thing."

Mrs. Parks always did. And when she fell down, she always got right back up.

## MRS. PARKS' HANDS WERE CREATOR'S HANDS

Mrs. Parks and I held hands a lot. We would sit silently and enjoy the moment, together, without words. The beauty of great friends is that you can be quiet in their presence. She didn't like shaking hands with people, only because her hands were so sensitive, and many people shook them too hard. Every time I look at a photograph of her hands, I remember how strong she was, and how she was able to express herself through her hands. She often said that we became good friends because she had never met anyone else with hands like hers. I hope as I get older my hands grow into hers. As you look through this book at Mrs. Parks' photographs, look at her hands. They are amazing grace.

Mrs. Parks' eyes were also sensitive, which was unfortunate for many people because she did not live during the age of smartphone cameras that do not require a flash to make a great photograph.

Often she would have to ask people not to take pictures of her inside (or at night when a flash was needed). She was always apologetic about this, and always explained why, so those who asked her were not hurt.

## Trust Is Greater Than Love

Mrs. Parks retained many friends from childhood. This was very important to her, and many visited frequently while she lived here. One of the most frequent childhood friends to visit was Johnnie Mae Carr, who she first met at Mrs. White's school. They began working together at the NAACP, where they were both to serve as secretary.

Mrs. Carr worked closely with Mrs. Parks on the Recy Taylor case, among others. Mrs. Carr favored the Octagon Room at The Mansion, because it had a large sunken tub with jets that soothed her arthritis. The two of them were so cute together, talking endlessly, but also, simply smiling as they held hands.

I learned during the decade Mrs. Parks was at The Mansion that she didn't keep all her friends…for a reason. She said, "When someone tries to get you to do something that is wrong, you must stand up for what you believe and move on."

She would always tell them why she was upset with their behavior, give them a chance to reform, and move on if they chose not to listen.

She said many times, "I'm in favor of any move to show that we are dissatisfied." But she would take this a step further. "The key is to open up your heart, to share your gifts and talents with your brothers and sisters in the world."

These simple words define how she survived with dignity: speak up—but speak with love in your heart. Not anger. Not hatred. She believed that if you talk about unity, if you focus your heart's work on love, you will reach more people.

Mrs. Parks believed that trust is greater than love in any relationship, whether it be family, community, religion, personal, as well as one's professional life.

Although Mrs. Parks sometimes had a blind spot toward her companions and caretakers, she was never reticent nor took a back seat as a symbol of the Civil Rights Movement, the Women's Movement, or the Human Rights Movement. She accepted her mantle with grace, strength, and fortitude. But she didn't believe being a figurehead was enough. Her focus was on changing people's hearts—and every day and every night she set out to do just that.

No matter what happened, she would always speak these words, "The struggle continues. The struggle continues. The struggle continues."

She would always shake her head when she said these words, at different times and during different experiences. But she would always say them with fire in her eyes and a purposeful smile on her angelic face.

A lot of promises were made to Mrs. Parks during her lifetime. Few were kept, but this did not stop her. She kept working to help others because it was what gave her life meaning. What she believed in was more important to her than how she was treated.

Mrs. Rosa Parks was more than the sum of things. While she continued to work quietly on her mission, she was not quiet. Her actions became more important than her words. In her autobiography, she eloquently wrote, "I understand that I am a symbol."

"Open your heart" was her message. "Now go out and change the world" was her call to action.

In several sections of this book, I allude that there were many people in Mrs. Parks' life—lawyers, family members, ministers, businessmen, people that worked at her institute and former friends—who tried to take advantage of her fame. Sometimes it took years for her to find out about their deceit. As soon as she did, she cut them off. I recall some of the people she asked for help to keep "those people" away from her. The women and men who loved and protected her many times did so at their own peril and at personal sacrifice.

Dealing with the people who attempted to benefit themselves from her notoriety made her physically and emotionally ill, and she knew she could not afford that toll on her mind, body, and soul, especially when she came into my life. I knew about this "syndrome," as Mother Parks and I talked about this on many occasions.

I distinctly remember one of our afternoon teas after I had just come home from the hospital after surgery. The essence of our talk was about how to heal your body by helping others. It made you forget about yourself, she reminded me. With friends around, she told me, you are protected from toxic people who have the gift of talk, but not the walk, those who are harmful to creators and givers as opposed to people who have an ulterior motive.

We often talked about how we were so much alike. When she alluded to this, I would feel overwhelmed, not quite understanding what she was saying. But when I finally understood the depth of what she was teaching, it became one of the most important lessons of my life: stay away from toxic people, even if you think you love them.

Let me make something clear, though. Mrs. Parks did not mind when people used her to learn lessons to better themselves. She did not mind when they worked together to make the world a better place. She did not mind when they raised money for their organizations using her name. However, she was adamant that they should be stopped if they were raising money at the expense of the children that she was trying to help. Or if they used her name to advertise for things that hurt children, like alcohol, drugs, or tobacco products.

Mrs. Parks with friends Virginia Durr (left) Fred Gray, and Johnnie Carr (right) at her Kennedy Center 77th birthday tribute, Washington D.C., 1990 (Photo: Library of Congress, 15045, No. 331)

She had been offered millions of dollars to do commercials and/or endorse products she didn't believe in, and she always said, "No." She never bothered to tell people why. She simply believed everyone would respect her mission more when she said no.

## A Channel for Good

Mrs. Parks was petite, weighing less than 100 pounds, but she was a tough cookie with a sweet inside. She had no tolerance for users or the proverbial wolves in sheep's clothing. She stood up to such types with the strength of a superhero.

Time after time, she was bemused when she heard that the bus she was supposedly riding on December 1, 1955 was being sold for large sums of money, with claims that it was "the one." A few times, she was even offered the "opportunity" to buy the bus being sold. She thought this was funny, as she said, "In my life I rode on every bus in Montgomery, so in essence, all the buses should be preserved."

She was saddened and frustrated that all the people and institutions that bought buses she supposedly rode on that fateful day had not instead donated money to help people in need. But she still loved seeing the buses fixed up and had no problem being photographed with "the bus." She understood the symbolism and importance.

She rarely said "no" to an appearance or the opportunity to meet people, especially children. She felt strongly that if people met her, then they would perhaps treat others they met with more love and dignity than they had before meeting with her.

Mrs. Parks tried to surround herself with selfless people who believed strongly in her mission. She could relax and have fun with them, go to a baseball game (a lifetime passion), go to dinner, or to a movie (she loved comedies), take them to church, or go with them to their church, synagogue, ashram, or mosque.

She loved to escape with her friends, extended family, and relatives. She kept praying for her brother's family that things would change in her relationship with them, even after he passed.

Freedom and justice are things you can work on, "But changing someone's heart, that's not up to you; that's up to them."

Mrs. Parks' devotion to faith, honesty, modesty, and courage made her what and who she became. She was one of the most moral people to ever grace my life. Her strong moral attributes are why so many people sought her wisdom and her presence.

Mrs. Parks' secret was accepting and understanding that it's all about saying "yes" to what God brings you. "We are all simply channels," she often said to me.

*I got your message, Mother Parks.*
*For as long as we live, we need to strive*
*not to be a Muslim in name,*
*a Christian in name,*
*a Jew in name,*

*a Buddhist in name.*
*We cannot fight for human dignity if we divine ourselves.*
*We need to all want to be counted with the disciples*
*We all need to try to walk in the footsteps of Mrs. Rosa Parks*
*and thus in the footsteps of the Master.*

Mrs. Parks studied many religions, not just her own, which was Methodist. She had many close friends of all ethnicities and religions. She did not just tolerate their beliefs and customs, she went to their ashram, their church, their synagogue, with them and studied with them, what they believed. She accepted and loved and learned from all.

## Life Lessons

Mrs. Parks was a role model for many people. She taught—by example—that you need to always ask questions to learn, no matter how old you are.

She loved going fishing as a child but had never learned to swim. At age 82, she took swimming lessons.

Mrs. Parks shared that when she was growing up in the South, African Americans were not allowed to learn to swim because White people did not want "Negroes" polluting the water they swam in. She felt that by learning to swim, she was making a statement to children of all colors that they have the right to learn and enjoy what all children do. She was also teaching that a person can learn things at any age.

Dare to learn to swim or learn something new—at any age. Learn things that make you happy. And always, have a reason for others to follow in your footsteps.

While she was completing *Dear Mrs. Parks,* she responded to one inquiry, "After I was robbed and attacked in my home in 1994 and knew I could have been killed, I recognized that God had another plan for me."

She also wrote, *"Each day I am granted, I use to the fullest. When my day comes, I will be bound for the Freedom Land."*

Mrs. Parks loved working on her computer during the last few years of her life. She insisted that children teach seniors at her institute how to use them. She believed that real freedom meant getting a great education, allowing you to rise beyond what you were born into.

When we flew together, I would sit next to her on the plane and write with her on my laptop. Few people had one at the time. She loved the size because it could fit in a purse and it wasn't too heavy. She would ask me hundreds of questions about the computer, and many times we would craft messages together on the plane.

She had hurt her hand during a fall that happened some time after her husband and mother passed, and it was painful for her to hold a pen. So, she would talk to me and we would craft short messages to send the people she was meeting with so they would have a memento of her thoughts. She had so much inside of her to say. I like to think that she would have loved the social media platforms of today because her message could connect with millions immediately.

Much of her strength came from her conviction in the authority of a supreme being, her Savior. Our friendship developed over our long conversations about God. One of our conversations became part of her response in *Dear Mrs. Parks*:

> *"I have been too busy living to be concerned about dying.*
> *I know God sees all and knows all and has a master plan*
> *for all to find their purpose.*
> *I do not question God's will, and I have served His purpose*
> *For what He wanted me to accomplish.*
> *Try to remember that death is as natural as living.*
> *God uses us all."*

She understood deeply that the world didn't revolve around her, but that her purpose was to serve her Creator.

Mrs. Parks was more than a symbol, she was—and remains—*Beyond the Bus*. She so firmly lived by the gem, "Life is not about living in the past; it's about today and fixing the future."

Mrs. Parks at various commencement ceremonies. She received more than forty honorary degrees in her lifetime. (Photos: Library of Congress, 47472, 2015649538, 2015649536, 38975)

## Become Her Messenger...She Would Like That

Mrs. Parks did not believe she owned anything or that she was owed anything. She lived to pass on messages about how to survive, how to live, and how to make life meaningful for others.

Mother Parks said that although certain laws for equality had passed during her lifetime, many people did not have equality in their hearts. But by speaking with children and focusing her energies on them, she believed this eventually would change. Children, she felt, just needed love and guidance along the way—just enough TLC to make a difference in their lives—and equality and unity would happen.

She also loved speaking before college students. At Spelman College in Atlanta, she is recorded as saying, "Don't give up. And don't say the movement is dead." I heard her say this repeatedly, to people of all ages. And I know she is watching over us all now, still repeating these words.

She told me one of the reasons she wrote *Dear Mrs. Parks* was because so many letters written to her were about the children fearing that because she was old, she would die. She addressed this in her book:

> *"Please do not fear what may happen to me.*
> *When I am faced with fear, I*
> *find comfort in the words of the Bible.*
> *When I feel afraid,*
> *I remember the Scripture my mother taught me:*
>
> > *-'Though I walk through the valley*
> > *of the shadow of death*
> > *I will fear no evil.*
> > *For thou art with me ...'*
>
> *This may help you find the courage*
> *to overcome fear when it is upon you.*

> *Remember—love—the love of your family,*
> *the love of your friends, the love of God.*
> *Love, not fear, must be our guide."*

She spent a lot of time trying to teach parents not to let their own fears seep into their children. She felt that with all the gun violence—especially in schools—it was important that parents remember to always make their children feel safe. She believed fear destroys; Love liberates.

In her letters, Mrs. Parks reminded children to not be fearful in their own homes, remembering her own experiences with the Ku Klux Klan when she was growing up. During those days in the South, the Klan could attack a Black person or family at any time without repercussion. But her grandparents always made her feel safe.

Mrs. Parks received thousands of letters from children around the world. Not only did she answer all of them, but she also saved them because they meant so much to her. Many were donated to the Library of Congress. If you wrote her a letter, visit the Library of Congress. You may find a piece of your own history there!

Mrs. Parks frequently received cards, letters, and notes from school children. (Photo: Library of Congress, 2015651085)

## Author to Author…Friend to Friend

Coincidentally, my first book was published while Mrs. Parks was living here. She had just finished *My Story* and was working on *Quiet Strength*. Sometimes, we would share what we were writing, discussing concepts, way-of-life thoughts, and the like.

The essence of Mrs. Parks' way of life was captured in words from my book, *The Simple Things*:

> *It's the simple things*
> *small steps*
> *the goals we choose*
> *the way of life*
> *we want to breathe.*
> *And I breathe*
> *because He*
> *has so many things*
> *for me to do.*

I could not have written that book had it not been for our many conversations over afternoon tea. I regret that I never got to thank her. I am sure if I had, she would have patted me on the hand as she often did, and said, "Lady H," as she often called me, "when you fall down, you get up." Then she would add, "It's okay. There is no need to thank me. It is I who thank you." That's who she was.

Mrs. Parks touched my life on so many levels during the ten years she graced my life. Although she did not physically take her pen in hand to write these words, I have a sense that she has been my co-author on everything I have done since she graced my door the first time.

Right to left: Elaine Steele, Luis Clavell, and Helena Zinkham, director for collections and services and chief of the Prints and Photographs Division of the Library of Congress, in 2014 reviewing documents included in the Rosa Parks Collection. (Photo: Library of Congress)

## IMAGINE THIS

I imagine this is the same truth that Luis Clavell found when he helped to curate a photographic exhibit, "Rosa Parks in Her Own Words," which opened at the Library of Congress (LOC) in 2019. A library program specialist at the LOC, Luis' mantra has been that the real story of Mrs. Parks must be communicated by as many people as possible —to as many people as possible.

"Her real time is now," Luis observed. "More than ever, she is needed to inspire all of us to be better people and to help others to help themselves." Without his strong suggestion, I would not have known that I had a book about Mrs. Parks in me, waiting to be revealed. His inspiration and love for her, discovering her life all over again while curating her exhibition, inspired both of us.

I wonder even now whether Mother Parks was speaking through Luis to urge me to write this.

## Lost and Found: Faith, Patience, and Endurance

In the middle of drafting this book, I lost it. I lost this book—not figuratively but literally. I have to admit, it was a trying, soul-searching time. My old computer kept shutting down and my IT guy told me I needed a new one. I did what I was told and bought a new one. But in transferring the information from the old computer to the new one, he forgot to make sure it automatically saved the manuscript as a Word™ document.

I had lost an intense three weeks of dedicated twelve-hour days. The work wasn't in the cloud, it wasn't on my desktop, and it wasn't backed up on our server. I even called a CIA "hacker" I knew for help. Nothing worked. The only thing that I could think to do was pray—not to find the book, but rather to discover why this had happened—again. Not why it happened technically—but what lesson our Lord was trying to teach me. Oddly, I was not angry, although I admit that I was upset and lost.

I was joined in prayer by four people I call my life changers: my husband Ted Spero; singer songwriter and recovery advocate Paul Williams; Luis Clavell at the Library of Congress; and Kathy Tait, the mother of Captain Scott Tait, a long-time friend of The Mansion and O Museum.

Each person, without hearing the response of the other three people, told me that Mrs. Parks was speaking to me, from above—still teaching lessons. I so believe that.

My husband gently told me, "Everything will right itself, as it should be. Let it go and begin again. There is a reason for everything. It's all okay. You need to get rid of the toxic people around you to write the loving book Mrs. Parks deserves."

Paul said: "It's not gone. The cyberspace shadow version is out-of-reach for the moment. The living, fluid magical evolving language, the prayer and play of your heart's memory, is expanding in formerly unseen detail. Wisdom distilled by your remarkable acceptance. This is exactly what you needed."

Paul wrote more encouragement, "You are capable of the magic, but it isn't really necessary. When it's time, let Mrs. Parks reveal herself to you. I would not try right now. I'd let my unconscious play with it a little longer. By the time you are ready to turn on your computer to write, let your fingers go to work, not your brain. You will find the book you are supposed to write is there, waiting for you to hear her. This is the kind of collaboration one would expect from Mrs. Parks and H. Leonards. This book is a heart song."

Luis said, "God is taking your words away, for good reason. You will soon understand His power and what a blessing this will be. Also, while you are learning this lesson though prayer, think about starting a scholarship fund for children to learn what you are teaching through your words. This is the way of our Lord."

Kathy said the most prophetic thing, which allowed me to be open, to listen, and to understand the real lessons and be open to Ted, Paul, and Luis' words. She told me, in front of her husband, son, and granddaughter, "God is telling you that you let pride get in the way of your message. God gave you one mouth and two ears. Think about why He gave us two ears. *Listen only to the loving people around you.* Listen to the words of our Lord." Boy, did she bring it home!

One of Mrs. Parks' favorite proverbs was from the Apocrypha, Ecclesiasticus 2:1–2 (*Oxford Study Bible*): *"…if you aspire to be a servant of the Lord prepare yourself for testing. Set a straight course and keep to it, and do not be dismayed in the face of adversity."*

On my second writing, the words formed new perspectives and chapters that are more forthright than the manuscript I lost. By losing my earlier draft, I found the courage to write things I had been afraid to disclose because I didn't know how to say them. In the second draft, I was able to step back and see a bigger picture.

Mrs. Parks taught me that no matter what happens, things happen for a reason. Reading the Bible—and listening—opens you up to giving more. Eventually, I became thankful for having lost three weeks of intense writing.

Mrs. Parks waits to board a bus at the end of the Montgomery, Alabama bus boycott, December 26, 1956. (Photo by Don Cravens, Getty Images)

What would my words be to her, today, after finally understanding that it was her essence that has inspired me to write this book? Thank you again and again Mother Parks, for all that you taught me, and all that you continue to teach. We need your lessons now, more than ever.

## A Family of Grand Ladies

From the time I started working at age 12, whenever I was asked in interviews what I wanted to be when I grew up, I always responded, "I want to be a grand old lady."

Mrs. Parks always insisted on being called "Missus." In turn, she never called anyone by their first name. She always used Mr. or Mrs. or Brother or Sister, and she always used their full name. She wanted to call me Miss or Mrs. H. Leonards, but found it odd that my name started with an initial. At the time, I was a single mother with a child. I did not like the title Ms., which I told her. So, for many months, she never spoke my name.

When she moved in, I wore clothes that I found fashionable at the time (the Annie Hall look): The tie, the pants, the hat, but with a more masculine bent, since I was having a challenging time getting bank loans.

Coincidentally, out of the blue, Mrs. Parks started calling me "Lady H." I smiled every time she said it, not connecting her moniker to my childhood goal of becoming a grand old lady.

Oddly enough, with her calling me Lady H, I stopped wearing ties and button-down shirts. I stopped wearing the professional pant suit and men's hats and started shopping at Salvation Army and Goodwill (and I still shop there!) where they always had midi length velvet dresses. I still dress in the same style that I did when Mrs. Parks lived with me.

I called them nun's outfits. Mrs. Parks and I would often laugh about that as I had told her that one of my early regrets in life was not joining a cloistered sect and becoming a nun.

## LOVE MATTERS

Mrs. Parks once told me, "Art, music, and writing are expressions of love. We are both loving people, although both of us love quietly, from afar, as we are both introverts." Perhaps because of this we both understand deeply that love has lasting effects. Love means not just giving to others — but also allowing our giving nature to receive from others.
Mrs. Parks, I am still learning from you. Love matters. Love is what matters. It's all that matters.

She would sometimes gently suggest I wear a purple or burgundy dress. Mrs. Parks always marveled at how well black velvet dresses traveled when we went on trips, I would have one small carry-on, while she traveled with as many as four checked bags on all our journeys.

Mrs. Parks' passion was shoes and hats and they all required seemingly endless luggage. Mrs. Parks owned a lot of shoes after she moved to Detroit. She had summer shoes, school shoes, winter shoes, church shoes, and even later in life, gym shoes. And, of course, bedroom slippers. She especially loved her bedroom slippers.

She kept everything in pristine condition. When she ran out of shoe racks, she kept them neatly arranged and labeled in shoe boxes under her bed.

The two of us became our own little family of grand ladies. Mrs. Parks told me that when she was growing up, no one really knew who they were related to, because enslaved family members often were separated. So "family" became whoever you were with at the moment. Perhaps this is another reason we bonded so easily.

As her "adopted" daughter, our bond ran deeper than friendship.

## Tea Parties and Lessons in Grace

Mrs. Parks loved entertaining friends at The Mansion. Nearly every year on her birthday, she would host a fabulous tea party for her friends, who would arrive from all parts of the world.

One Sunday afternoon, during one of Mrs. Parks' birthday tea parties, a couple across the street called the police constantly about a party that "was disturbing the peace." When the police didn't come immediately to investigate, they added this to their complaint, "People of another color are breaking into The Mansion at 2020 O Street." A police officer who came to the scene told me this.

The police dispatched six cars and left them double parked in the street, several with their flashers on. When the officers entered, they found eighty of Mrs. Parks' closest friends, mostly elderly, all wearing pill-box hats and white gloves, having tea. When everyone's initial embarrassment subsided (the policemen, Mrs. Parks, and her guests), the officers had a memorable time meeting their most gracious host, Mrs. Rosa Parks.

After "the incident," I apologized to Mrs. Parks for my racist neighbor's behavior. Mrs. Parks turned to me and said, "Dear, this is okay. When those

### 50 CENTS A DAY

Mrs. Parks worked as a field hand when she was six years old. She was given a flour sack, like the other children, and was expected to pick at least one pound of cotton a day. She would make picking cotton a game by seeing who could pick more. When Mrs. Parks was in her early teens, she picked cotton sometimes and chopped cotton at other times. She was paid 50 cents a day. She worked barefoot, as did all the children who worked in the fields. All these things that she endured as a small child informed the way she lived as an adult. I think this is why she loved shoes so much.

## COMMUNITY

Community was important to Mrs. Parks. Her family strived always to be one community. If one family had food, everyone in the community shared it. She told me that so many times they came together at church, in their homes, and at work to help each other. Times were very hard, but "we didn't think so because we didn't know we were poor at the time."

people go to sell their house, you need to buy it for me. That's how you deal with racism."

Some years later, I did just that. And that's how the Rosa Parks Safehouse came about as lodging and vacationing facility. I was inspired by her words:

*"We can expand our vision to include the universe and the diversity of its people, or we can remain narrow and shallow and isolate those who are unfamiliar."*

Mrs. Parks' grace superseded karma. In finding truth, answers come in different forms, at different times.

### Understanding May Come Slowly

About three years after meeting Mrs. Parks, I finally got the courage to ask her why she chose the small room as her bedroom, rather than the bigger one that Ms. Steele stayed in. She replied, "My dear Lady H, Elaine is much more important than I am!"

The look on my face (my mouth dropping, my eyebrows raised) must have surprised her. She chuckled, thought for a long moment, and then in measured

Dr. Douglas Brinkley signed book, with dedication (Photo: O Museum in The Mansion)

words said, "I am Mrs. Rosa Parks, but my daughter does all the work."

Brother Willis said to me many times, "H, you don't understand how important it is that you opened your heart to Mrs. Parks." I didn't at the time—and not for many years later. I do now. I understand deeply what I didn't know then.

Sometimes, you have to wonder what God's plan is. But always, He is doing the right thing, just sometimes, it takes us a while to understand.

Dr. Martin Luther King, Jr. stands with Mrs. Parks at a dinner given in her honor during the Southern Christian Leadership Conference convention in 1965. The Montgomery bus boycott thrust Dr. King to national prominence in the Civil Rights Movement. (Photo: Bettman Collection via Getty Images)

## Quiet Strength

Mrs. Parks taught me that the beauty of great friends is that you can be quiet in their presence. During our best moments together, we would just sit next to each other, saying nothing, simply feeling the moment. Other times, actually most times, when someone talked or I would ask her a question, she would not answer right away. She measured the few words she spoke.

I believe that this characteristic of choosing words carefully, ensuring that the message is truly heard, was what made her most endearing. I also think on a deeper level that is why she has lovingly endured as the "Mother of the Civil Rights Movement," when at the time other people may have been more famous.

We each have our own way, our own mode of survival, our own path to salvation, our own view of our mission, our own notion on religion, our own unique fingerprints, our own choice of how we respond to the cards we are dealt.

These were Mrs. Parks' lessons. They are the reasons why she will always endure as a beacon of light and a name people will remember into future generations.

All around The Mansion are original letters that Mrs. Parks wrote and lots of memorabilia. If you visit, here are some of what you will see.

Look for the autobiography of Mrs. Parks, co-written by Dr. Douglas Brinkley, just outside the Amnesia Room on the first floor. Many of the interviews in the book were conducted at The Mansion.

On the second floor, there are more displays with pictures and letters. She used to sit on a sofa in the reception room nearly every day and greet guests who came to visit. They had no idea they would get to meet her. Because privacy was so important to her, we never told anyone that she lived here.

On the same floor, The Mediterranean Room was another one of her "hangouts" because it was easy for her to access and is filled with comfortable white sofas. A picture of Mrs. Parks hangs in The

Mediterranean Room in her honor. On the same floor is an elaborate chess table that Cicely Tyson and Miles Davis often dined on. Davis loved this room because of the acoustics, created by the combination of a teak soaking tub, teak double sinks, a marble floor, and lots of mirrors.

Across the street, in the Rosa Parks Safehouse (the building that I bought and turned into more lodging space, as she had urged) hangs one of Mrs. Parks' many honorary degrees, this one from the University of Southern California. She was always so gracious in receiving such honors, but especially from a university that she could not have attended. Also in the safehouse is a limited-edition print of her on the bus that her good friend, Artis Lane, created and donated to us.

People from all over the world come to stay at the Safehouse and enjoy its amenities. The property features seven bedrooms and features accommodations with a shared kitchen and a shared lounge.

## Mrs. Rosa Parks and OutKast

In 1999, my son, Z was 14 and into rap music. He heard the OutKast song about Mrs. Parks and became upset. He went directly to where she was sitting at the bay window of the reception room, on a beautiful blue tapestry Victorian sofa and said, "Mrs. Parks, I love rap music and I love OutKast's songs. They don't say bad words about you, but they use words that should not be associated with you. It's not right."

Mrs. Parks asked if he could play it for her. My son turned bright red and stammered, "Maybe I could just give you a cassette tape so you can hear the song on our own."

She agreed, "That sounds good," with a huge grin on her face. He would have been embarrassed to hear the words in the song in Mrs. Parks presence.

Later, we found out that her lawyer sued OutKast, the record label, LaFace, and parent company, BMG. The initial case was dismissed, and the case was appealed and denied on First Amendment grounds.

When Mrs. Parks was in California visiting friends, she told them how upset she was at having lost and why. They introduced her to an attorney named Johnny Cochran, who took her case *pro bono*.

Cochran's legal team appealed the case, and in 2003, the US Court of Appeals for the Sixth District allowed him to proceed with the lawsuit. The lawsuit was settled in 2005, after Mrs. Parks' death. In the settlement, OutKast, their producer, and labels paid an undisclosed cash settlement and agreed to work with the Rosa and Raymond Parks Institute for Self-Development on educational programs about the life of Rosa Parks.

While this is another example of how a child can make a difference, just as important, it's an example of Mrs. Parks' inner strength. The courts said no to her twice, the case first being dismissed, then being denied again based on the grounds of free speech. But she knew that she was right, so she simply didn't take no for an answer.

Mrs. Parks took the long view of what was right and wrong. This was not always easy for her nor financially beneficial. But always, she kept the end in mind. She taught positive lessons in all her behaviors. She never backed down given the choice of right and wrong.

This case was groundbreaking for intellectual property rights and publicity rights. Again, Ms. Parks was a trailblazer.

And my son? He became a lawyer. Perhaps the desire to study and practice law started with Mrs. Parks and OutKast. I like to think so. You never know how people influence you, on so many different levels, all the time. I know he deeply loved her.

## The Rebuke

Mrs. Parks was always quiet, gentle, and kind. She only spoke when she had something to say. Her answers were measured, filled with wisdom. But she was firm in her resolve and in her focus.

I was raised in a very strict environment. I was taught not to speak unless spoken to. I was also taught to always call older women Miss or Mrs., and to always called men "Mister or Mr." But as I got older and left home, I stopped with most surname formalities.

When I was introduced to Mrs. Parks, I was asked to always refer to her as "Mrs." Not just to her, but when referring to her among my friends or associates.

Then one day, I accidentally called her by her first name. She looked up at me, quite surprised. As always, she thought for a while, and responded in a very quiet, but firm voice. "My name is Mrs. Rosa Parks."

I mumbled my apologies. Mrs. Parks just smiled gently back at me. No words were necessary. I did not ask why to her or anyone else on her team. It was what was right for her. I respected that.

Years later, when I was first working on this book, I was in Detroit for a Rock & Roll Hall of Fame Board Retreat. I invited Elaine Steele's sister, Anita Peek, to lunch at the Foundation Hotel where my husband and I were staying. I finally got the nerve to ask her why Mrs. Parks didn't like her first name and shared the story about her gentle rebuke when I called her "Rosa."

Ms. Peek said, "Oh, Mrs. Parks loved her first name. And she loved her grandmother Rose, who she was named after." What she told me next stunned me. Again, I had been naïve and uninformed.

She said, "You have to understand that in the South, slaves did not have last names. Most could not get marriage certificates."

So, to be legally married was of great pride to Mrs. Parks. Not only did she love her husband deeply but being called Mrs. gave her dignity and self-respect. She went on to explain to me that having a last name was significant because during Slavery so many Black people didn't have them, or they simply took the name of their enslaver.

She was so proud to be married to "Parks." Even when he was no longer alive, she loved and honored him, speaking about him lovingly every chance she got.

## A Passion for Baseball

Mrs. Parks was not athletic, but she told me she loved to play stickball as a child. She then transferred these wonderful memories to a passion for professional baseball. As a young woman, whenever possible, she attended baseball games. She especially liked seeing Negro Leagues Baseball games. One time, she went to the Negro Leagues' annual East-West All-Star game and sat with several of the original players in this league. Being there was a highlight for her. The league even gave her a NLB jacket to wear, which she treasured.[6]

Mrs. Parks' favorite player was Jackie Robinson. She talked about him frequently when she met with children and used him as an example to teach them right from wrong. She said he should be known—not just for being the first African American to play in Major League Baseball—but also because he understood the bigger picture of being an exemplary role model in his personal life. His doing the right thing, being a family man, and knowing right from wrong was important to Mrs. Parks. She admired him greatly for this.

Mrs. Parks once signed a baseball for Curt Flood, an African-American outfielder (1956–1971) for the Cincinnati Reds, the St. Louis Cardinals, and the Washington Senators. Flood, encouraged by the Black activism of the Civil Rights Movement and the call for Black Power, took a major step and challenged baseball's reserve system, taking his case to the US Supreme Court in 1972. Although Flood lost his case, his challenge is credited with opening the door that laid the foundation for free agency in baseball. Two names, one ball, and so much history.

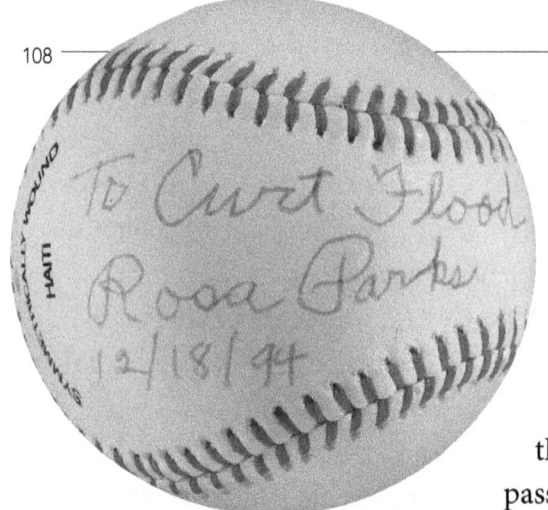

From one pioneer to another, a signed baseball. (Photo: Henry Ford Museum, Detroit, and Library of Congress

## MRS. PARKS' GOLDEN RULE

Faith, honesty, modesty, and courage are the four foundations of life.

Mrs. Parks' love of the game did not just stop with her personal love. She often paid for tickets to bring children to baseball games in Detroit. Whenever possible, her institute in Detroit continues with this tradition today.

### Her Golden Rules

In her teachings and in her books, Mrs. Parks emphasized the importance of leading an exemplary life. She said, "When a decision is made, it should be decided on the basis of what is right, not because it is a popular thing to do."

Mrs. Parks understood from childhood, partly due to the lessons her grandparents instilled in her growing up, how important it is to live above reproach. She had always tried to live an exemplary way of life, but it wasn't until after she was arrested that she understood the depth of its importance.

She explained in *Rosa Parks: My Story*, and in other accounts that she had no police record (up until that point). "I worked all my life [since age six]. I wasn't pregnant like the first person who refused to give up her seat." Mrs. Parks was referencing Claudette Colvin, who at age 15, had been arrested for refusing to give up her 'White' seat on a Montgomery bus several months before Mrs. Parks. The NAACP did not get behind Ms. Colvin's case, however. One reason may be because the judge in her case had dropped the charges of disturbing the peace and violating the city's segregation law. She was charged as a juvenile and convicted of the sole charge of assault against a police officer during her arrest. (In 2021, a Montgomery juvenile court judge approved Ms.

Colvin's request to expunge the court record. At age 82, Ms. Colvin's record was expunged, and she is no longer a juvenile delinquent.)[7]

Had the NAACP gotten behind Ms. Colvin and appealed her case, it would not have advanced the organization's cause since the segregation law violation had been dropped. Local Black leaders did use the Colvin case to attempt to gain ground for better treatment on buses. Also, several months after her arrest, Ms. Colvin became pregnant. An unwed, pregnant teen who had a reputation for being outspoken was regarded as a less-than-ideal candidate.

Conversely, Mrs. Parks being older, employed, and established, was believed to have the maturity necessary to withstand the pressures that would most certainly accompany a challenge to Montgomery's segregation laws. Plus, Mrs. Parks had experience working with the NAACP and had taken social justice leadership classes at Highlander Folk School in Tennessee.

I sat through many meetings that she held with famous people who weren't leading exemplary lives; one I will never forget. When we left the meeting, Mrs. Parks was shaking her head in sadness. Later she shared with me, "I am so sorry for his family. I know by his body language that he won't change his behavior and won't follow through with my suggestions. He doesn't understand how important it is to be a role model for young boys and girls, let alone his own children." She then paused for a long time before saying, "He will not change his behavior and get back on the right path. Sadly, there is nothing more I can do to help him."

Although she spent time with the man's wife and children after that, she never met with him again. And she was right. I watched the pain this man brought upon his family a few years later by his behavior. In the end, it was he who was hurt the most. He didn't just lose his family over his lifestyle, he lost his job, his self-respect, and later went to prison because of how he tried to finance that lifestyle.

## The Jack of Hearts

Mrs. Parks read the Bible daily. She used the jack of hearts playing card as a placeholder, which in Tarot is the sacrificial love card. It symbolizes an honest young man in love, often away, but committed and sincere, and would make good marriage material.

It's also called the "Christ Card," as when it is placed at the very center of the spreads, the lines form a cross. As one of the "fixed cards," the jack of hearts provides no recourse. Those with the card must stay the course until they learn to love unconditionally to master their intense emotions.

The reason Mrs. Parks used this card as her bookmark was because the jack of hearts represents their greatest fulfillment on a spiritual path. You can see her Bible with this card inserted in it when you visit the Library of Congress exhibit, *Mrs. Rosa Parks: In Her Own Words*.

## Proverbs

Mrs. Parks learned right from wrong from her mother, her grandparents, and the Bible. They also taught her about prayer. Later, because she knew that many children didn't know what doing the right thing meant, she would teach by example what her mentors and teachers taught her.

She would always say that whenever you are not sure what to do, "read your Bible." Many times, I heard her tell children to read Proverbs because they were easy to read and understand. She would say that the book taught you not just the way of our Lord, but even how to choose the right friends.

She was a woman of great faith. She understood the spirituality of humility. Her word was her bond. She never went back on a promise or a commitment. Throughout her long and blessed life, she denied herself comfort so she could serve others. She believed in something much more important: human dignity.

But Mrs. Parks could get discouraged at times, just like you and me. She said to me many times that some days it was very hard to keep going when "all our work seems to be in vain." Mrs. Parks recounted "things" that had happened, but no one had heard about them because they weren't reported. She was overwhelmed by all the violence and hatred she witnessed, experienced, or heard about, but she never gave up—ever. In *My Story*, she wrote: "There is nothing to do, but keep going."

I earnestly believe her determination to keep going and stay positive was her belief, which she often reiterated, that all the important words in *Webster's Dictionary* had five or fewer letters in them—words like love, hope, give, enjoy, trust, faith, and gift. She lived those words rather than wallowing in unpleasant events.

When bad things happened, Mrs. Parks would take a pause to gather inner strength, but she always turned her emotions into action. This was another of her leadership skills: When you are overwhelmed, step back, pause for however long it takes. Then come back with a vengeance—not with anger, but with love, and keep on putting one step in front of the other.

"God has given us all free will," she wrote. "He lets us all make our own decisions. And when people treat us mean or try to hurt us, God gives us the strength to overcome."[8]

Mrs. Parks just didn't deny herself, she picked up a cross. Not the cross like people wear dangling from their ears or around their neck but the true cross, the heavy albatross that represents rejection from most of society. She was a housekeeper, a hostess, a secretary, and a seamstress—in all these positions she demonstrated grace, competence, and courtesy. And when she was out of work for her defiant actions, she helped organize food lines to feed those even less fortunate than she.

She was accused, nameless, and faceless, and brought before courts of law on unjust charges. In the Montgomery newspapers, Mrs. Parks was never named in the early accounts of the arrest. When she refused to give up her seat, the White newspapers wrote "a Negro seamstress was arrested …."

When the press in the North picked up her mantle and gave her a face and name, she and her husband again lost their jobs and were unable to find new ones because potential employers thought they were trouble. Because of the death threats and lack of work, they were forced to move to Detroit in the hopes of starting a new life. But because of her fame, she and her husband again could not get work.

She moved (her beloved Parks and her mother stayed behind) from Detroit to Hampton Institute in Virginia to work at a hotel as a hostess, although that name really meant she was a glorified maid. She could not get a job anywhere else, and she needed to help support her husband and mother.

When Dr. King was stabbed and nearly died, she recalled that she went into despair and returned to Detroit. Yet, she took the time before she left to write a handwritten note to the president of the company where she was working: "Thank you for giving me this job. I must return to my family now." It was these little things she did that endeared her to everyone.

Whatever happens that we think is the worst possible thing, it's not. Mrs. Parks taught that there is always something that someone else considers worse. All we can do is continue to work so that others can be helped.

A letter from the Business Office at Hampton Institute (now Hampton University) in Hampton, Va., confirming Mrs. Parks' salary in 1958 as hostess of the Holly Tree Inn, the campus residence and guest house . Following the Montgomery Bus Boycott, Mrs. Parks and her husband, Raymond, had difficulty finding employment. She worked at Hampton a little more than a year before returning to Detroit to be with her husband and mother. (Photo: Library of Congress, mss859430297)

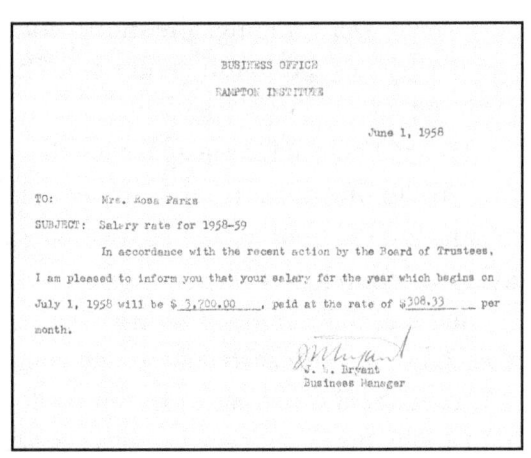

## Gospel Brunch Sundays

About six months after Mrs. Parks arrived, she began to heal spiritually and physically. It was then she suggested we host the gospel brunches on the first Sunday of every month. This was amazing to me—and so thoughtful—because I would never have asked her if we could do this.

Her idea was the start of the most delightful events we have ever held here. While the brunches helped bring attention to The Mansion as a venue, their deeper message was that healing can occur through music and storytelling.

Music historically has been a driving force in the movement for racial equality, instilling hope and pride in all who were committed to the endeavor. Mrs. Parks understood this importance more than anyone I have ever met.

She said she learned this from spending so much time with her great friend Harry Belafonte, who had told her that by promoting human rights through music and storytelling, systematic racism—and disparity—could be addressed. His conceptualization of the "We Are the World" famine relief project cast light on the importance of music in changing the world. USA for Africa, the organization that spearheaded distribution of the largesse from this song, has donated more than $100 million to fight hunger.

Watching Mrs. Parks listen to gospel music was joyous. While the performers were singing, she didn't hold conversations with anyone, and her friends did not interrupt her. They could sense her rapture in the moment.

Mrs. Parks loved the gospel brunches, which were attended by seventy-five to one hundred and fifty people each month. Always partial to Sundays, she used to take delight in dressing up for each event. Plus, she loved church and church music.

She especially enjoyed eating healthy, fresh food, which we served at each event. With each course, she would request a take-out box and put what she did not eat in her purse for later. She never ate a lot of food at one time, and she also never wasted anything.

Mrs. Parks always insisted on lots of vegan and vegetarian options. She loved sweets, especially all types of cakes and cookies. But she was disciplined. She would always eat the desserts later, in her room, after her meal had been properly digested. We used to joke about it. I would always remark that I wished I could be more like her in my eating habits. Perhaps this is why Mrs. Parks weighed less than 100 pounds and I weigh so much more!

Most of the performers at these brunches came from local churches, and a few came from other parts of the country. I will never forget the time when a group from Nashville was performing for Mrs. Parks and Emmylou Harris was staying with us at The Mansion that weekend. The music moved the singer so much that she stood at her chair and started singing with the performers. Someone sitting next to me leaned over and said, "H, your neighbors are so talented." I didn't bother to tell her that Emmylou was a legendary, Grammy Award-winning singer and songwriter, but both Mrs. Parks and Emmylou had a great long laugh when I told them later.

Mrs. Parks, surrounded by friends and guests at The Mansion, ca. 1997 (Photo: O Street Museum in The Mansion)

## Coming Full Circle

One of the lessons Mrs. Parks taught me was that sometimes you have to say things repeatedly, so that people understand what you really mean. Here goes.

For several years, I had some rather contentious disagreements with some racist neighbors who were upset that I held events to which African Americans were invited. They also didn't like the fact that I had Black board members. One of those neighbors, who was then president of one of the neighborhood associations, expressed his displeasure by putting two rats in my face during a meeting that had been scheduled as an attempt to bring reconciliation to the issue in the community.

Brother Willis told me Mrs. Parks was quite upset when he told her about the head of the neighborhood association shoving rats in my face. He knew her well enough to know that she would talk to me privately about this at a later time.

A few years later, during one of our afternoon teas, we were discussing a group of soldiers to whom she had just spoken. She said she understood why I had passed out and ended up in the hospital because of the rat incident. I felt very uncomfortable at first when she said this. When ugly things happen to you, you don't want to remember them. I told her that. Even writing about this these many years later makes me queasy.

It was then that she opened up to me about her having been raped during the attack in her Detroit home, although she didn't use the word. She usually used the words "accosted" or "assaulted," which are not as explicit. But the description, her hesitating, carefully chosen words, her breathing, her hands, expressed even more pain—piercing our time together.

She also talked about why she had gotten involved with documenting Black women who were rape victims while she was in Alabama. She told me why the Recy Taylor rape case was so important to her, and

> *I had been pushed around ~~for~~ all my life ~~____~~ and felt at this moment that I couldn't take it anymore. When I asked the policeman why we ~~were~~ had to be pushed around? He said he didn't know. "The law is the law. You are under arrest." ~~I ____ I went to____~~ I didn't resist.*

In this portion of a note written by Mrs. Parks (circa 1956–1958), she reflects on her feelings on December 1, 1955, the day she refused to surrender her seat to a White passenger. It was a decision for which she was subsequently arrested, but which also sparked a movement that received worldwide attention. The complete letter, along with other memorabilia, are available for viewing at the Library of Congress website, *loc.gov*. (Photo: Rosa Parks Papers, Manuscript Division, Library of Congress, mss859430226)

---

This QR code links to Mrs. Parks' handwritten account of an assault attempt upon her when she was 18 years old. From the Library of Congress (*loc.gov*) collection, "Mrs. Rosa Parks: In Her Own Words."

how she learned that no matter what happened to her, someone else was worse off than she was. This is how Mrs. Parks survived. She believed the only way to survive was to help others talk about what they were feeling. The reason she was able to document rape victims was because the people she talked to knew what she had endured.

But she said after the first "incident" (which was an attempted rape), whether future violations were directed at her or those she loved, the feelings would surface again and again, and that she had to learn to modulate her reactions, learn to differentiate the degree of deception with which she was confronted. For example, if someone lied to her, or cheated their family, she needed to step back and say, "I will not judge you. I must forgive you. But I don't want you around me or I will not be able to continue with my mission."

Mrs. Parks taught me the only way to beat the devil is not to play with him. Instead, use bad experiences to learn positive lessons and remember that you are not the center of the universe. Whenever I get flashbacks of our conversations or my own experiences, I repeat these lessons, so I can go forward.

She said the hatred she had encountered made even minor infractions appear bigger than they were. This was important for me to hear—and yes, relive. She was opening up to me because she saw how upset I still was and wanted to reach out and help me, like I had helped her just by being around a corner of her life, giving the sanctuary she and her friends needed, at no cost.

When confronted by mean-spirited people, I remember these conversations I had with Mrs. Parks.

## The Remarkable Human Will

I have debated whether I wanted to write this, as I have only talked about what Mrs. Parks told me with a handful of people whom I deeply trust and admire. Circling back to those still alive, only one person said I should not write this because they knew that this was a difficult issue for me and didn't want me to end up in the hospital from the pain that will come when these facts become public.

Still today, I also continue to use other words to describe bad things. Most everyone does. It doesn't matter how old you are, your race, what religion you practice, or your country of origin—ugly is ugly. It's simply too painful to dredge up images, buried so deep inside.

While Mrs. Parks didn't ask me to be silent, I believed she wanted me to protect her privacy. But then I think, why would she have talked to me on several occasions about "this" if she didn't want me to tell her story? And why, if her team told me she wanted her privacy protected, would she ask me to host monthly gospel brunches in her name?

Dr. Douglas Brinkley told me that while co-writing Mrs. Parks' autobiography, one of the few changes she requested was that he not describe her husband as an alcoholic; but rather, someone who drank heavily. Still, she told him it was his decision. She saw no difference between the truth of the two descriptions—the latter was simply gentler.

So, bringing up what Mrs. Parks told me, exposing these ugly incidents has been agony. I don't write these things without physical and emotional pain and anguish. It's not easy writing about assault, but when it's about a hero and your mentor and beloved mother, it's even more difficult. Still, I know I must tell the story. This book is about truth…and Mrs. Parks was about truth.

I truly believe that my initial manuscript was "lost" because I did not share this story about Mrs. Parks. I now know I needed to be honest and write the whole truth about her life, not just the manicured stories. As I wrote, I felt her reaching out to me from above to dictate what she had not written. I firmly believe she wants girls and women

Mrs. Parks speaking at the Poor People's March at Washington Monument and Lincoln Memorial, Washington D.C., 1968 (Photo: Library of Congress, 2017650273)

to know that they too can lift themselves after painful things happen—and perhaps become the Mrs. Rosa Parks of their generation.

According to statistics from the Centers for Disease Control and Prevention, nearly one in five women have experienced a completed or an attempted rape during their lifetime. These women need community. They need communion and hope.

The human will is truly amazing. Time after time, it has triumphed against unbelievable odds. But it's not the once in a lifetime dramatic, visible, up-by-the-bootstraps effort that brings enduring success. It's day to day, putting first things first.

## Mrs. Parks' Struggle for Social Justice

I know Mrs. Parks' heart and soul and I firmly believe that if she were alive today, she would have written another book titled *My Story: Stories I Have Been Afraid to Tell*. I am confident that Mrs. Parks would be a vocal supporter of the #MeToo Movement and that she would have been more candid about what she had suffered.

Why do I say this, how do I know this? Mrs. Parks was a trailblazer on so many different levels, for more than seventy years:

- She traveled throughout the South in the 1930s to document the stories of Black rape victims.

- In 1944, Mrs. Parks investigated the rape of Recy Taylor, a 24-year-old wife, mother, and sharecropper in Abbeville, Alabama. She then founded the "Committee for Equal Justice for Recy Taylor." This case became the catalyst for Black women's civil rights resistance.

- She brought people of all races into the NAACP during the 1950s.

- On December 1, 1955, she refused to give up her seat and move to the back of the bus.
- In the 1960's, she protested against the Vietnam War.
- In the late 1960s, she referred to Malcolm X as her personal hero.
- In 1968, she lobbied for Black reparations.
- In 1969, she went on record for showing the similarities of police harassment in Montgomery with what was happening in Detroit.
- In 1970, she spoke vehemently in support of helping to free the Soledad Brothers.
- During the early 1970s, she started wearing African-inspired clothing when speaking before young children to show them her pride in her African-American heritage.
- In the mid-1970s, she taught recycling at her institute.
- In 1972, when Angela Davis was released from jail, Mrs. Parks was the first person to invite her to speak—introducing her before 12,000 people.[9]
- In 1979, she created the Joanne Little Defense Fund to support the first woman in US history to be acquitted using the defense that she used deadly force to resist sexual assault. The case was recognized in legal circles as being a pioneer in scientific jury selection.
- In 1991, she testified against Justice Clarence Thomas during his Supreme Court confirmation hearings, focusing on his dismal civil rights record.

Right: Mrs. Parks at the March on Washington, August 28, 1963
(Photo: ©Bob Adelman) Used by permission

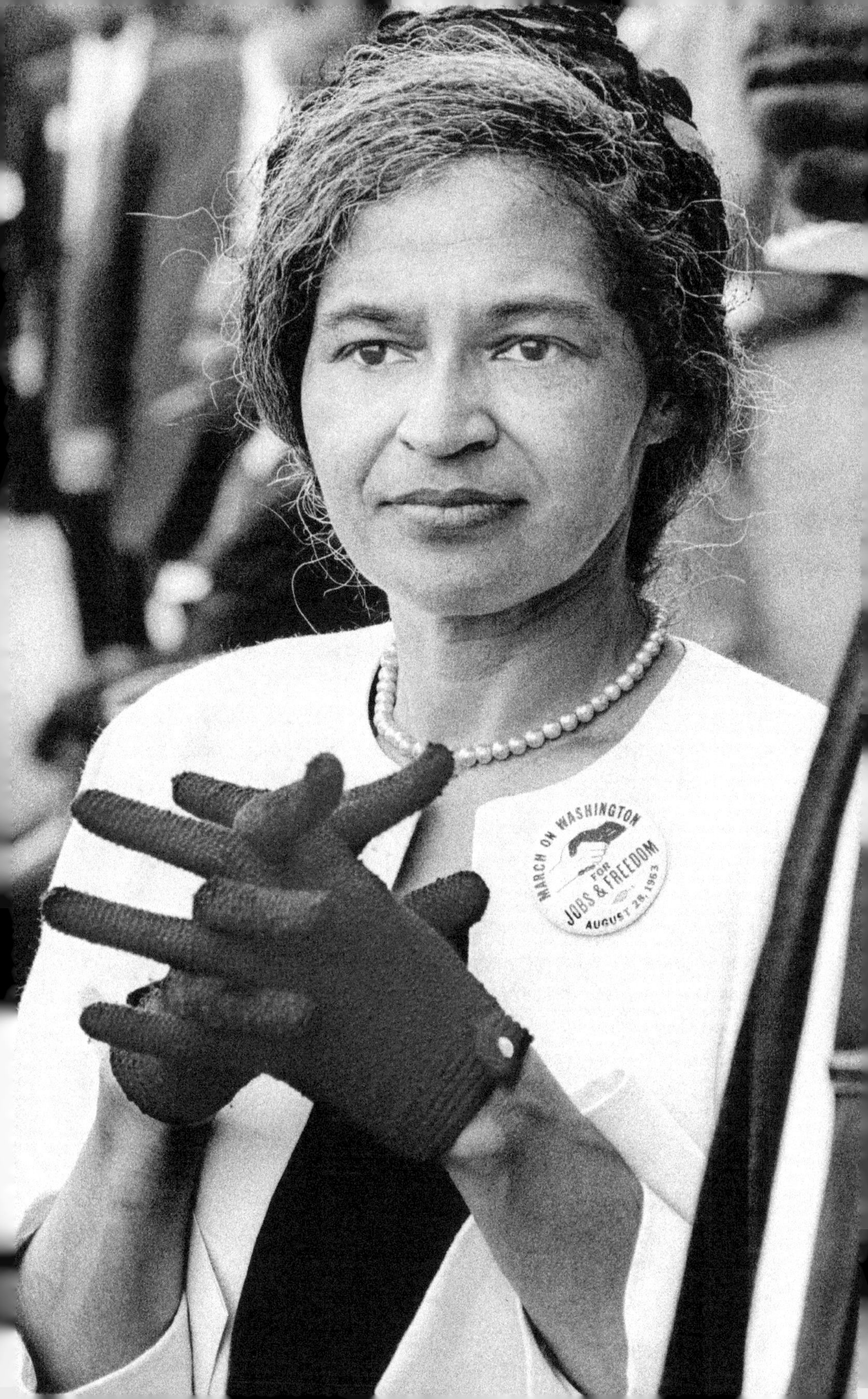
MARCH ON WASHINGTON
FOR
JOBS & FREEDOM
AUGUST 28, 1963

- In 1999, she became the first African-American woman to be awarded the Congressional Medal of Honor and the Presidential Medal of Freedom.
- In 2003, she requested that the Nation of Islam's Minister Louis Farrakhan speak at her funeral.
- In 2005, she was the first woman and first African American to lie in state inside the US Capitol rotunda.

## MOTHER OF THE CIVIL RIGHTS THE MOVEMENT; GRANDMOTHER OF THE WOMEN'S RIGHTS MOVEMENT

*Editor's Note:* The information provided in this story is the author's account based on her interactions with two historic figures—Mrs. Rosa Parks and Dr. Dorothy Irene Height. Despite specific details of what happened during the March on Washington, various historical accounts corroborate that gender politics was a factor in the noticeable absence of women addressing the audience from the platform.

None of the official speeches during the march was offered by a woman. Before the official program began, entertainer Josephine Baker gave a speech. Otherwise, women speakers in the official program were invited to offer a "tribute," led by organizer Bayard Rustin. Daisy Bates (mentor and supporter to the Little Rock Nine students who integrated Central High School in Little Rock, Arkansas) spoke briefly during the tribute, offering less than two hundred words. Mrs. Bates was a replacement speaker for Myrlie Evers, whose husband Medgar recently had been murdered for his work as a civil rights activist. During the tribute, Diane Nash, Prince E. Lee, Rosa Parks, and Gloria Richardson were introduced.

The male organizers of the event had claimed the omission was due to the "difficulty of finding a single woman to speak without causing serious problems vis-à-vis other women and women's groups"[10]

Mrs. Parks challenged boundaries her entire life. She should be remembered for more than just one incident—although it was pivotal. For nearly her entire life, she was the cutting edge of history. She was always respectful, but she was a warrior against an unjust social order.

As President Clinton aptly said at her funeral, "She made America a better place to live, but she did not make America good."

That's up to us.

---

At a planning meeting held a few days before the event, Anna Arnold Hedgeman (the only woman on the planning team) had offered a statement that read, in part: "In light of the role of Negro women in the struggle for freedom and especially in light of the extra burden they have carried because of the castration of our Negro men in this culture, it is incredible that no woman should appear as a speaker at the historic March on Washington Meeting at the Lincoln Memorial...."[11]

Activist Gloria Richardson was slated to give a two-minute speech; however, by the time she arrived at the stage, the chair with her name on it had been removed. The event marshal took her microphone away after she said "Hello." Ms. Richardson, Mrs. Parks, and actress/singer Lena Horne were escorted from the podium prior to Dr. Martin Luther King's speech.[12]

Even though they were intentionally excluded, women played a critical and pivotal role during the course of events of the largest human rights march in American history. Women all over America helped to organize and raise money for the event. Gospel singer Mahalia Jackson offered the last musical performance prior to Dr. King's speech, and was positioned near the podium when she shouted, "Tell them about the dream, Martin!"

At her admonition, Dr. King set aside his prepared notes and improvised the next section of his speech[13] to what is famously regarded as his "I Have a Dream" speech.

Women played a major role in bringing the 1963 March on Washington to fruition, from planning to raising money to attending the March on August 28. Yet, their voices were excluded from the platform on the day of the event. (Photo: Warren K Leffler, Universal History Archive/Getty Images)

Mrs. Parks was pained when women, who were early organizers of the Civil Rights Movement, weren't recognized at events or rallies—or even asked to speak.

She initially understood the men's concern about having women on the podium. In the 1960s, major television networks began covering their rallies. The men had said they feared the women might be targeted for rape, as they had always been in the South had they been profiled. Mrs. Parks believed that the women involved should have been allowed to make that judgment call, not the men. Being recognized in public was a conscious choice she made. She understood the consequences well.

"Seek first to understand, then to be understood" was her motto. She understood why, and had deep compassion; nevertheless, she wanted to be accepted—and treated—as an equal.

Mrs. Parks was particularly upset when the women, who came from all over the world to Washington DC for the 1963 March on Washington for Jobs and Freedom, were not allowed to participate—even though they comprised three-quarters of those marching and had helped organize it. The only woman allowed at the podium was Joan Baez, who sang with Bob Dylan. To his credit, Dylan had refused to go on stage unless Baez accompanied him.

Dr. Dorothy Height and Mrs. Parks told me that among the notable women not allowed near the podium when Dr. King delivered his famous speech were Twyla Tharp, Josephine Baker, and Mahalia Jackson. Not even Dr. King's wife, Coretta Scott King, was near the podium.

After much protesting, the male organizers did allow these women to stage a march in another area (after the main protest was over). They named this rally the "Negro Women's March for Freedom." But

## SEIZE OPPORTUNIY

"I wish I could be here with you today, my dear friend, but unfortunately my age does not permit such a trip at this time. So, I am sending this missive through my daughter, H. H. Leonards.

"We have both endured much in our pasts, but, as we know, the past cannot be changed. So it is with this knowledge, we look to the future, and to a better world for our children.

"This is what we have done. Lifted ourselves up from the prisons of the world and let imagination and inspiration, our quest for equality, be the hope of others.

This is a blessing God bestows upon us. Life, my friend, is too short not to seize each opportunity, with an open heart."

for this program also, men did the speaking. The women were only allowed on stage to sing. When Lena Horne chose to say the word "Freedom" before she began singing, the microphone was pulled from her hands, and she was escorted—by Black men—off the stage.

Perhaps the worst slight was that no women were invited to be part of the delegation of ten leaders that met with President John F. Kennedy after the March (to discuss the Civil Rights Act). Even Mrs. Parks' close friend, Anna Hedgeman, the woman on the 1963 March planning committee, was not invited. This was not a public event. All the excuses the men gave for women not being front and center were thus unacceptable.

Dr. Height, Mrs. Parks' close friend (and a frequent guest of The Mansion and the O Museum) and president of the National Council of Negro Women, observed, "I've never seen a more immovable force. We could not get women's participation taken seriously by these men."

Ms. Hedgeman indignantly said about Mrs. Parks after this march, "They did not include Mrs. Rosa Parks or the rest of us who were responsible for that day." She went on to note, "Women were left to find their way home."

Mrs. Parks told me she was dumbfounded and told her friends she hoped for a "better day coming." The experience of the march, compounded by the marginalization for women's roles in the Civil Rights Movement, made her more resolute to work for human rights for all. Not just civil rights for a few.

On many occasions Mrs. Parks said that through her experiences she grew stronger, more resolute. She knew that she had to stay positive, or change would not happen. She understood that there are different forms of betrayal. She didn't overreact. She told herself to smile, and as she did her eyes began to shine with more purpose.

From that moment on, the rights of all people became the focus of her life.

## BE POSITIVE, ALWAYS. FOCUS ONLY ON GOOD

How she presented herself helped her focus on her mission. She was proud of her femininity—she just didn't want her gender to keep her message from being heard. She also never dressed down because she didn't want other people to use her appearance as an excuse not to listen or understand her vision. While men of color were not treated with dignity, women (of any color) were not respected as leaders or visionaries. That bothered her.

## "I Love You"

We were in Los Angeles for Brother Willis' birthday, and we went to his church to pray and to celebrate with him. Part of going to church—and often the Black Church experience—with Mrs. Parks, Elaine Steele, and Brother Willis included socializing afterward. This Sunday, the fellowship was more memorable than usual.

After the service, Mrs. Parks and I were outside talking with Brother Willis and a few of his friends from church. An elderly gentleman came up to us and Brother Willis gave him a big hug, and said, "Brother, how are you doing?"

He hugged Willis back and said, "I love you."

Brother Willis introduced us to the man as his uncle. We shook hands and he smiled impishly and said to each of us, "I love you."

Willis continued to talk about the sermon, the day, about Mrs. Parks, and with everything Willis said, his uncle responded, "I love you." They were the only words he spoke, but he spoke them to us repeatedly.

I thought this was beautiful. It was a joyous few minutes. Then his uncle turned from us and began talking to other people nearby.

When his uncle was out of earshot, Brother Willis explained, "My uncle was an abusive man…never had anything nice to say to anyone. He beat his wife and was simply an awful man. But she stayed with him. That was the thing you did then. Since he had a stroke, the only words he has been able to say are, "I love you."

Mrs. Parks remarked, "How beautiful! God does work in mysterious ways."

## Mrs. Parks and Nelson Mandela

In 1990, Nelson Mandela, South Africa's anti-apartheid hero, was released from prison.

That same year, he chose Detroit as his first stop in the United States because, as he later explained, Mrs. Parks' act of courage had inspired him while he was in prison. As he stepped off the airplane to the platform where the stairs began, he saw a long line of dignitaries, led by Detroit's first African-American mayor, Coleman Young.

Mrs. Parks had been closer to the front before the plane arrived, but everyone had been jockeying for a prime position. By the time Mr. Mandela and his wife, Winifred, stepped from the plane, Mrs. Parks and Elaine Steele had been shuffled near the back of the crowd.

He searched the crowd but did not immediately see Mrs. Parks—the very woman he had come to Detroit to meet. He raised up his arm at the top of the airplane stairs and started yelling the name, "Rosa Parks! Rosa Parks!" Soon the crowd caught on and thousands of people started yelling her name. Someone in the front of the line went back to bring Mrs. Parks back to the front. When Mr. Mandela saw her, he and his wife descended the stairs to embrace her.

He hugged her and said, "You sustained me in prison for all those years." It was a remarkable moment.

A few years later, Mrs. Parks was invited to his 80th birthday celebration in London, England. She asked me to go on her behalf, as

Detroit Mayor Coleman Young (left) looks on as Winnie Mandela hugs Mrs. Parks, with her husband, Nelson Mandela, in the background during the couple's 1990 visit to the United States. (Photo: David Turnley/Corbis/VCG via Getty Images)

she was not feeling well enough to make this trip. I read her missive to him. A portion of her gracious letter to him read:

"*I wish I could be here with you today my dear friend, but unfortunately my ages does not permit such a trip at this time. So I am sending this missive through my daughter, H. H. Leonards.*

*We have both endured much in our pasts, but as we know the past cannot be changed. So it is with this knowledge, we look to the future and to a better world for our children.*

*This is what we have done, lifted ourselves up from the prisons of the world and let imagination and inspiration, our quest for equality, be the hope of others.*"

## Taking Care of Little Things

Mrs. Parks had endured health problems from the time she was a little girl. But from 1955 on, she began to have serious stomach issues, and before it was fashionable, she became a vegetarian. She was always a trailblazer in whatever she did.

Her diet was very important to her. She never drank any form of alcohol. She wanted to stay healthy. She ate small meals five times a day and was very careful how much and what she ate. She was not a fussy eater, just a careful one.

Her favorite foods were broccoli, greens, sweet potatoes, and string beans. She also talked about nutrition and frequently discussed the importance of recycling—at her institute. She'd had vegetable gardens behind her home where the children who attended the institute learned how to grow fresh vegetables. She lived to be ninety-two and attributed her long life to eating right.

The cutest thing was dining out with her because no matter what she ordered, she barely ate half of it, and always asked for a to-go bag, putting it carefully in her purse. She never wasted a morsel. She knew what it was like not to have a good meal to eat.

Mrs. Parks seldom wore make-up, but when she did, she glowed. Elaine Steele's task was to apply just the right amount to enhance her delicate features for television, but never too much to obscure in her own natural beauty.

Mrs. Parks did not cut her hair for the last twenty years of her life. She was very fair-skinned, and had long, soft flowing hair. It grew so long that it cascaded down her entire back when we unbraided it. Sometimes I got to braid her hair, and wrap it around her head, like a crown of light. For me, it was an honor.

Each year she grew older, her skin became smoother, as soft as a newborn baby. She was an angel, and she looked like one.

Mrs. Parks loved to go to the movies. She particularly loved comedies. When she laughed, when she smiled, she lit up the room.

The one possession Mrs. Parks took great pride in—other than her Bible, letters from Dr. King, and one from Malcolm X—was her shoe collection. Having gone barefoot so many years growing up, she took such great pride in being able to buy shoes, and just as important to her, to take care of them. She always kept her shoes in pristine condition. In fact, she kept all her clothes in pristine condition, but she especially loved her shoes. Every time she wore a pair, she wrote copious notes about what else she wore and what she was doing that day.

Mrs. Parks easily could have made a lot of money during her lifetime. She was smart. She was beautiful. She was famous. But she chose to utilize the funds she raised—or was given—for the good of others. Even during the Montgomery Bus Boycott, when she was out of a job, when someone paid her for a speaking engagement, she used the honorarium to feed those who were less fortunate.

### Keep the End in Mind

No one could use Mrs. Parks' past or present against her to derail her cause. I believe it was due to her innate ability to balance everything that happened to her with the ability to forgive others for what had been done to her. She also had the ability to forgive herself when she made mistakes and then learn from them.

She was able to compartmentalize her experiences to keep from being overwhelmed or annihilated by them. She knew the only thing she could do when bad things continued to happen was to stay focused on her mission, vision, and values—and always help others. She didn't always have control over what happened to her, but she always had a choice in how to respond. She took considerable pride in how she chose to be.

I imagine the reason that she dressed so properly and meticulously was to be beyond reproach. She loved hats, gloves, jewelry, and shoes, yet how she dressed and how she carried herself were never flashy. Her appearance was who she was inside—regal, understated, and pure with purpose. She felt, and rightly so, that how she dressed, how she presented herself, helped her succeed in her mission.

Later in life she felt this was so important that she taught deportment and how to dress for success at her institute. She loved these classes because she knew how much they helped others. She also knew that even though some people thought this was such a small step, it was an important one. For her, perception was reality.

## Live a Positive Life

Mrs. Parks was assaulted throughout her life both physically and emotionally, but she never used this as an excuse to stop living, nor did she allow anything to defeat her spirit. She believed that there are hidden blessings in everything God gives; that being a giving person means you become more open, more giving to others…that pain and fear are illusions of choice. "It's simple," she would always say, "When you fall down you get up."

Mrs. Parks incorporated prayer into her everyday life. She felt the importance of believing in something bigger than yourself, which to her meant God.

Mrs. Parks wanted to be an author and she was driven by her desire to help children and women. The books she wrote confirmed her interest as well. She used this dream to write about and to document their plight for the NAACP.

She authored four books, all or parts of three of them while she lived here. I like to think that both of us influenced each other as we wrote. All of Mrs. Parks' books became my personal favorites. It was like a parent's relationship with her children. You tell each one they are your favorite, and they are.

Mrs. Parks once told me, "I can't change what is inside someone. That's something they have to do themselves." Living according to this principle, she let go and forgave everyone she loved. She used the pain she felt throughout her life as a motivator. She chose to champion constructive change in our justice system.

Still, with all that she was involved in, there was nothing Mrs. Parks would not do for her brother, Sylvester. She loved him deeply, and thus, she loved all his children, without judgment. She had moved

Mrs. Rosa Parks and her mother, Leona McCauley, 1978 (Photo: Library of Congress, 2015648740)

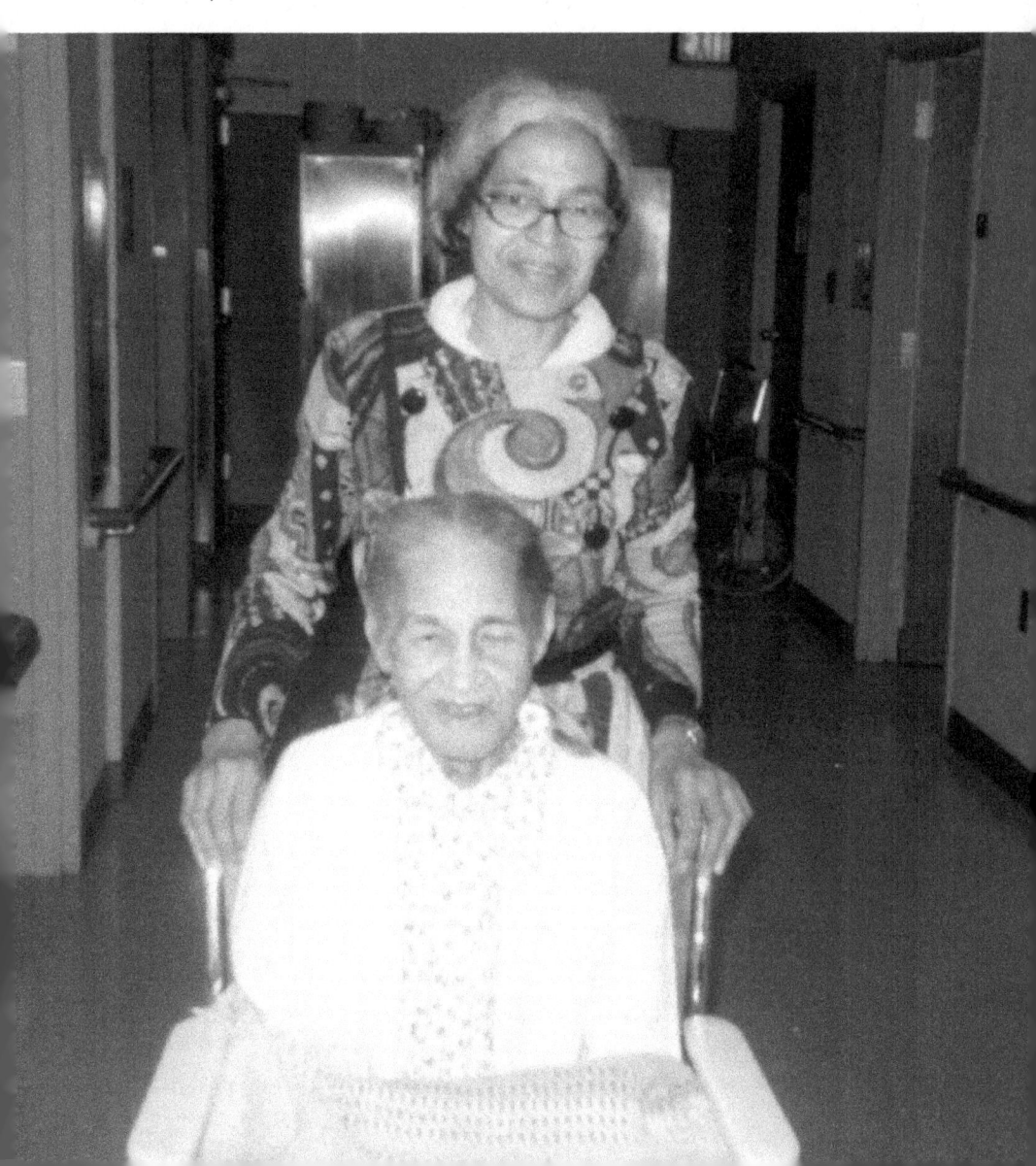

to Detroit to be with him. They spent two to three days a week together there. Her husband and her brother were great friends as well. They even worked together. But after Sylvester died, his wife and his thirteen children were not always around. "Perhaps this will change one day," she said, repeatedly, as if it was a prayer.

Mrs. Parks was disheartened by some family members who didn't return the respect and love she gave them. She never said no to her brother's children when asked for money or for her to write letters on their behalf. But it saddened her that after Sylvester died some of his children only spent time with her when they wanted something. Although they were "blood," they didn't always treat each other like family, she often lamented.

Even though Mrs. Parks worried that certain relatives might sue her estate after she died, she still hoped that one day they would see the light and pick up her mission to do the right thing. She was rightly concerned that some relatives would sue to capture her estate; she was wrong that they would choose to do what she believed was right.

Twenty years before her passing, she had tried to adopt her best friend and companion, Elaine Steele, so she would have a "legal" child for purposes of ensuring that her financial legacy was used for the right purposes. But Elaine's mother, who was alive at the time, refused to go along with her wishes.

Mrs. Parks made a video so her brother's family would know how much she loved them, but she wanted her personal property to go to Elaine, and her intellectual property to go to her beloved Institute.

She knew, before she knew.

I was struck with great sadness to hear what was happening almost immediately after her death. A lawsuit was filed against her estate. Brother Willis called to tell me.

On the journey between Washington D.C. and Detroit, with Mrs. Parks' body on the plane, one of the nephews passed by my husband and me at our seats and said to someone with him, "Why are those White people on this flight?" It was a devastating comment because we knew Mrs. Parks never saw color. I remembered her saying, "We are not born to judge, only absorb and create." I said nothing.

Mrs. Parks strongly believed that no one is wrong if they allow love to come into their hearts. She had so much love in her heart and gave so much love to everyone. Life is filled with many curve balls and irregular turns, but Ms. Parks always said to take the long view of what is right.

She so strongly believed that love had no color and that we all are created by the same God. Mrs. Parks always said it didn't matter what you believed, as long as you believed in something bigger than yourself. Fame doesn't keep you from pain and suffering. Now, looking back at what has transpired since Mrs. Parks passed, I understand the sequence of passage, and God's bigger plan, above human frailty and failings. Everything that happened to Mrs. Parks during her life and after was meant to happen, and in the sequence it did.

## Grace Supersedes Karma

Mrs. Parks believed that the thirst for knowledge appears when you are ready to learn. She believed that you lift everyone if you share your struggles. She believed you must think beyond where you are.

But she also knew that you can't confuse being friendly with having a friendship. She believed that family isn't necessarily those who share your DNA. She also knew from her grandparents that during slavery no one had any relatives, and if they found out they had some, they were separated immediately. From that she knew that family meant community, in the broadest sense. She knew that gifts come from the heart, not the pocketbook. And she knew that sometimes things just happen.

And when they do, they can become defining moments that we use to recalibrate who we want to become: such as the boycott, like the marches, like deciding not to move from her seat on the bus, like being kind to the man who was fingerprinting her, like dealing with her blood family members who didn't understand how important it is to love all humanity. Mrs. Parks understood defining moments more than anyone I have met.

After her husband and brother died in 1977, she fell on black ice near her home in Detroit and broke two bones. She needed a long break to replenish her soul and body, so she moved into a nursing home to be with her mother. She came back even stronger. That's when she created The Rosa and Raymond Parks Institute for Self-Development (RRPI). She wanted to contribute to others. And she wanted to honor her beloved husband with the dignity that he so richly deserved by including his name.

Mrs. Parks did not turn away from defining moments—no matter how painful they were. She utilized them to propel her forward and to fulfill her mission, fully. After her assault, when I first met her, she was driven even more.

Thirteen years after her passing, the courts finally awarded her estate to RRPI.

## Dreams Transform Reality

Because her father had abandoned his family, I imagine Mrs. Parks was afraid of not just marriage, but also any relationship. She writes in *My Story* that she hid from Parks when he first asked for her mother's permission to see her. He loved and respected her from the moment that he saw her through his barbershop window.

She fell deeply in love with Parks. He was older and heavily involved with groups that wanted to make the world a better place. He had no fear. He didn't care if he was accepted. He wanted justice for anyone who suffered. And he loved and cared for his mother and

## THE ONLY WAY OUT IS THROUGH

"I experienced problems and pain just like everyone else. I have learned throughout my life that what really matters is not whether we have problems, but how we go through them. We must keep on going to make it through whatever we are facing. The only way out is through."

Mrs. Rosa Parks, *Quiet Strength*

his grandmother, a thing that her own father had not done. In addition, Parks made Mrs. Parks his priority.

Parks loved her every day that they were together. He also loved her when she was away and fully supported her need to travel. Indeed, she had to be away from him many times. For them to survive financially after the bus incident, she had to leave her husband and mother in Detroit to take a job that would provide for them. First, she accepted a job in Virginia in 1957. She was very lonely there but didn't complain. It was a job. Later in life, she traveled extensively for civil rights events and rallies.

She felt safe and protected being married to Parks, but at the same time, she felt free being married to him. Her marriage to Parks gave her freedom to become her own person—freedom to honor him, not just as husband and wife, but also as equal partners. She often expressed that she didn't feel comfortable with the fact that the press only talked about her, ignoring her husband.

Theirs was an unusual relationship. They married in the 1950s, a time when most women were homemakers. It was a time when Black women, when pregnant, were not seen in public. She was always a trailblazer.

Raymond Parks, ca. 1947
(Photo: Library of Congress, 013.00.00)

She understood, on many levels, what her husband felt—not because he complained (much like her), but because so many times Mrs. Parks' peers and the politicians would not allow her to speak or relegated her to the back of the crowd to glorify themselves. She never did this to her husband. She acknowledged him wherever she went, even if he wasn't with her. She knew what it felt like to be marginalized.

Even after he died, she spoke about him in public. He always had her back. He was her flame and her one true love. Everything she did, she did in his honor.

## Learn Positive Lessons from Everything

In the ten years Mrs. Parks stayed at The Mansion, I never saw her be disrespectful to anyone. She treated those who waited on her the same way she treated the Pope or the president of the United States.

What I did see, however, was how she was consistently hurt by the behavior of her brother's children. I knew there were issues with some of them while she lived with me. I saw her write her brother's family handwritten letters inviting them to every holiday, to nearly every special event where she was honored, and to her birthday party each year both here and in Detroit. They seldom accepted her invitations, her overtures toward reconciliation, or her desire to be inclusive, unless they wanted something (usually money or a favor).

She never complained to me about them, but many times I saw her wince when Brother Willis would say one of them had just called her. She would dutifully get up to answer the phone. But her step was heavy. Every time she would leave the room to talk to them, he would mumble under his breath and pace the room until she returned. When she would reenter, he would always make sure she was okay.

But the real quandary for me was her relationship with her father. She talked about her relatives, on Parks' side, with such love, but she never said a word about her father or her brother's progeny.

I learned that Mrs. Parks didn't see or hear from her father from the age of 5 until she was in her late thirties. I was told that he tried to reach out to her because from his standpoint she had become famous. I also was told one of the greatest sadnesses that Mrs. Parks experienced was that he never tried to see her brother, Sylvester, unless she was present. She told me her brother was obsessed with wondering about James McCauley, just as any small boy who had been abandoned by his father would be.

Her father started writing letters to her in Detroit, but she knew the handwriting wasn't his because her mother told her he could neither read nor write. They both wondered who was writing the flowery looking letters. Was it a daughter of his they didn't know about or his new girlfriend or wife?

Then she got a letter from her father with many misspellings and bad grammar, but powerful just the same. This letter is on exhibit at the Library of Congress.

He hadn't signed it, "Your father, James" or "Your loving father James." He just signed it, "James."

Mrs. Parks spoke to her mother about it and she talked at length with her brother. For the sake of Sylvester, she finally agreed to meet him. They met in her home. Raymond, Sylvester, and her mother were present. She forgave him, but she kept her distance, being polite, but

Rosa and Raymond Parks standing in front of an automobile, most likely in Detroit, 1970 (Photo: Library of Congress, 15045, No. 262)

> May 15, 1950.
> Patterson Calif
>
> My Dear Daughter
>  I Received Your letter of May 5th, a few days a-go and was indeed Glad to hear from you. and the others that go to make up the family. and to learn that all was well. and that Sylvester was married and doing well. was indeed a Pleasure.
>  Jes I wrote to sister Jessie Bell. at Eufaula Ala. first. she informed me of Deaths. of mother Bro Robert and George. I also wrote to sister Addie at Ozark, and inquired of you. she said you was still in Montgomery but failed to give me your street adrss. in her first letter but did so in her second one. I keept thinking of writing you, and still putting it off. it was in view of the fact that I was over shadowed. with open shame. that I and I alone a-llowed the Evil spirit to lead me Completly out of myself

A portion of a letter to Mrs. Parks from her father, James McCauley, in 1950, expressing remorse for having abandoned his young family. (Photo: Library of Congress, 022.00.0) not hugging him, ever. Just as when Mrs. Parks was a small girl, she was dutiful, kind, gentle, and always trying to do the right thing. Her love for her brother was absolute, so she reconciled with her father for his sake.

We are registered for this course in life, whether we signed up for it or not. The book of life is not just the one we have lived, but also everyone else's books we have felt. Once you hear out loud what you fear most, your fears evaporate. Once you express your truth, negative and damaging results rarely occur.

Getting fears and bad things into the open is never a sign of ultimate truth, even if at the moment it seems like your truth. It is simply one of the steps, but not the end. I am sad, but not saddened. When you understand this, you are never depressed.

Never complain about how you are treated; instead, do something positive about it.

## She Had to Help

On September 3, 1944, Recy Taylor, a 24-year-old mother and sharecropper, was walking home from her church in Abbeville, Alabama when she was abducted and gang-raped by six White men. Mrs. Rosa Parks insisted that she be the one to investigate this on behalf of the NAACP. Her report received extensive coverage in the Black press. Indictments were issued against the accused.

In the film, *The Rape of Recy Taylor*, director Nancy Buirski explores Taylor's story, Mrs. Parks' work on her behalf, and the history of racial violence, particularly against Black women, in the postwar South. In her book *At the Dark End of the Street*, Danielle L. McGuire writes: "After World War I, the Alabama Klan unleashed a wave of terror designed to return 'uppity' African Americans to their proper place in the segregated social order."[13]

Although she had written about rape in the South during the 1930s, it was against that backdrop that Mrs. Parks documented

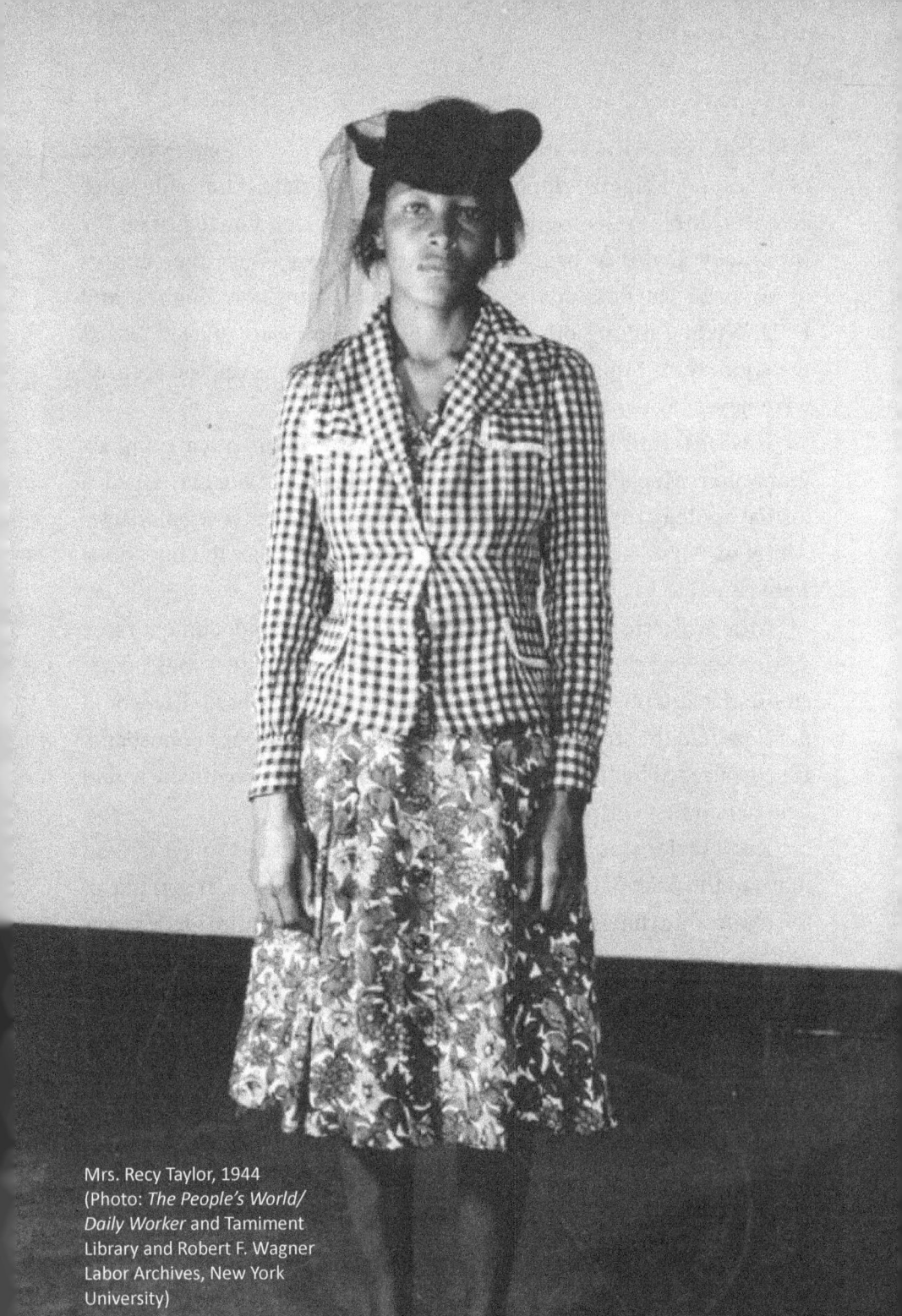

Mrs. Recy Taylor, 1944
(Photo: *The People's World/Daily Worker* and Tamiment Library and Robert F. Wagner Labor Archives, New York University)

evidence, took witness statements, and sought justice for the victims of widespread bigotry rippling throughout the state. Alongside other activists, Mrs. Parks founded the Committee for Equal Justice for Mrs. Recy Taylor to bring attention to the case. With the support of W. E. B. Du Bois, Mary Church Terrell, Langston Hughes, and E. D. Nixon, among others, eighteen chapters were started across the country and this case rose to prominence. However, the accused were never brought to justice.

It wasn't until 2011—more than sixty years after the case and six years after Mrs. Parks passed—that the state of Alabama issued a formal apology to Taylor for her treatment by the state's legal system. Although Mrs. Parks fought for reparations during her lifetime, none were issued to Ms. Taylor's family.

Mrs. Parks shared with me how difficult it was to document these stories. She said she could document them, but the toll they took on her emotional and physical well-being was exceptionally hard. She would not have had the strength to continue had it not been for her husband. He encouraged her to pursue these cases, knowing it eventually would help her come to grips with her own experiences.

Recy Taylor was raped in 1944. Mrs. Parks' refusal to get up and move to the back of the bus happened eleven years later. This is one of the frustrating things for Mrs. Parks throughout her entire life. She was put in a box where the only thing people knew was her act of defiance December 1, 1955. This is another reason why I believe that Mrs. Parks was the grandmother of the Women's Rights Movement, and that if she had lived a few years longer, she would have written a book about her involvement in giving African-American rape victims a voice and come out publicly with her personal stories of being defiled.

Sometimes our justice system doesn't get things right, but eventually, the laws can come around to be just. But Mrs. Parks said they only come around if you change people's hearts. How do you do that? You tell the truth.

## Forgiveness Is a Gift

Mrs. Parks understood that a person who doesn't forgive can never move forward. She was filled with boundless wisdom, yet she had bottomless grief in her personal life.

She always told me that forgiveness is a gift, that you must forgive everyone—of any and everything—to embrace life, to give back. Most of all, you must forgive yourself.

She often would say that failure to let go of negative feelings does not make them go away; instead, it magnifies them and creates illness in the body. She would say, "Heal your soul and your body will follow." She lived by this creed and adapted proverb: Walk in like a lamb. Walk out like a lion.

## Meeting Pope John Paul II

On January 26, 1999, Pope John Paul II made a whirlwind trip to St. Louis. Mrs. Parks, Brother Edwards, and Elaine Steele were staying at The Mansion when I first heard of his visit. I told Brother Willis that I thought it would be great if Mrs. Parks could meet with him. He talked with Mrs. Parks, who told him in her succinct manner, "That would be very nice."

Two days later, Mrs. Parks was invited to meet the Pope in St. Louis. She asked the three of us to attend with her. Brother Willis was the magic man. I don't know how he managed to get a meeting with the Pope in just two days, but he didn't stop there. Brother Willis somehow secured free flights for us all as well as complimentary hotel accommodations in St. Louis.

Mrs. Parks asked me to sit next to her on the plane to St. Louis. At the beginning of the flight, we simply held hands. Her hands were soft and warm. When we held hands, it was always like holding the hands of an angel. Halfway through the flight, she turned to me, "I need your help. I want to write something to the Pope and read it to him. It has to be short because I can't write long letters. My hands hurt too much."

"Mrs. Parks, I never thought of saying anything to the Pope," I told her. "I just thought it was amazing that we would have the opportunity to meet him. I am awestruck. I get to be with you and meet the Pope!" This was doubly exciting for me, as I am a devout Catholic. "I have about thirty crosses in my purse that I hope he will bless."

She looked at me for a long time. She did not laugh or even smile. She also didn't judge me. She looked down at our clasped hands and after a time she said, "Lady H, you have to understand. When God gives you the opportunity to speak to anyone to get your message out, you have to seize the moment." We sat in silence for some time, still holding hands. Then she said, "When you have these miracles presented to you, you must rise up to the occasion and be a messenger for what is right." I thought a lot about these moments with her as I pulled out my small Sony laptop.

I wasn't nervous. I didn't even think about what Mrs. Parks was going to say. I just became her, for a few moments. I think it was her hand in mine that helped me. Or it might have been her telling me why it was important.

I wrote a simple message, as I knew she would want: "As a most respected, honored, and great leader of this world, I ask your patience to address racism with your words and example."

In measured soft words, Mrs. Parks said, "He is not a great leader."

I replied, "But Mrs. Parks, he is the Pope. I am Catholic, and to me, he is a great man!"

She thought for a long while and said, "No one should be called out as a great leader. We are all great men and women. Let's use the words moral leader." Again, I knew she was right.

When we got to the hotel in St. Louis, Mrs. Parks sat at the desk in her room, and asked me to read aloud what I had written. I would read a few words at a time, and she would write them in a notecard. When we were finished, she put her note in an envelope, wrote his name on the front, and put it in one of the books she had written, *Quiet Strength*.

While we were waiting to meet the Pope, Mrs. Parks asked me what she should do when we arrived at the meeting. Neither of us knew the protocol of meeting the Pope, but I suggested that when the "pages" or "ushers" or "butlers" (I did not know what they were called) took us to meet him, they would tell us what to do. But I advised that she should be herself first and foremost and do what she thought was best.

I told her that she was an amazing, strong woman and that her message to him was clear and more important than protocol. I also said that no matter what the pages told her to do, she should be bold. This was her moment.

When they came to get us at our hotel, she asked to use her wheelchair until the Pope arrived because she was tired from the trip. They wheeled her to where she was to meet the Pope in his private quarters, which were impressively spacious. Brother Willis, Elaine, and her friend from Detroit, Craig Burton, were all with us. They placed us at the end of a large ostentatious hall.

They told Mrs. Parks that the Pope would come to her, and that she should not walk up to him. There were no chairs. At the anointed (pun intended) time, two large, heavy sounding doors opened. Mrs. Parks usually did not like people seeing her in a wheelchair, but she was very tired from her trip and stayed seated. A processional arrived. Cardinals and bishops came in single file to pay her homage.

The first priest was from Africa. He walked toward her, about twenty-five feet from the doors. When he got to just a few feet away from her, he kneeled to the floor, stretched forward, and kissed her feet. I could not hold back my tears. I was so overwhelmed with emotion from this gesture. Time stopped for me, and still does every time I remember this moment.

Mrs. Parks smiled and motioned for him to stand. He did, but then bowed again, kneeling this time, and kissing her outstretched hands. His gesture of respect and love made everything after that anticlimactic. Our private meeting with the Pope was not as powerful as this moment, although the outcome of the meeting was more significant for people around the world.

After he left the room, other bishops and cardinals came to greet her. It was a very long processional. When the line ended, we were alone again in the big hall. Then, the heavy doors at the end of the room reopened and the Pope entered. He was wearing heavily bejeweled vestments and leaning on a big staff as he walked very slowly toward us.

Mrs. Parks was told many times to stay where she was. She turned to me and said, "Help me get out of my wheelchair. I want to walk to the Pope." I did as she requested, without question, but just before I put my hands under her arm to help her up, I dropped the wad of crosses I had in my hand for the Pope to bless. The sound of them hitting the floor pierced the solemnity of the moment. Mr. Willis picked them up and quietly handed them to me. We all followed Mrs. Parks quietly and reverently.

As we got closer to the Pope, we saw why Mrs. Parks did not follow protocol. Even from a distance, Mrs. Parks could tell that every step forward was agony for him. He was so appreciative that she came to him. Although she had mobility challenges as well, when she saw him, she didn't think about herself. Following are the words of the letter, which she read to him while holding her book. Then she gently gave him her letter and book.

*"Peace and blessings be upon you.*
*I pray for your health and strength,*
*and I ask that you pray for mine.*

*My lifetime mission has always been simple:*
*that all men and women are created equal*
*under the eyes of our Lord.*

*But the issue of racism still plagues our world.*
*It is a cancer that has troubled me—and others—throughout my life.*
*As a most respected, honored, and moral leader of this world,*

*I ask your patience to address racism with your words and example."*

*Mrs. Rosa Parks*

The next morning, Mrs. Parks and Pope John Paul II held a joint press interview on racism in America.

When I read the news report to her on the plane coming home, out of ignorance, I neglected to thank her for giving me the experience that allowed me to write this. She simply patted my hand and smiled. I sigh as I write this, as I can still see that smile and feel her hand in mine. Now, all these years later I get the opportunity to publicly thank her for being my muse.

On the plane going to meet the Pope, I was in awe, and I didn't think beyond that. Mrs. Parks did. Not only did she think about what she would say, she also took time to record her thoughts in a short, hand-written note that she knew he would keep and refer to over the years.

It wasn't just that what she said to him had made such an impact, it was the whole package. She came to him, so he would not have to walk so far, even though she had risen from a wheelchair. She asked him to speak the next day with her at a press conference. Of course, he could not say no. No one could say no to Mrs. Parks when she asked, although she didn't ask as frequently as she could have.

Mrs. Parks reading her letter to Pope John Paul II in 1999, with Elaine Steele and H. H. Leonards (Photo: O Street Museum in The Mansion)

Pope John Paul II didn't hold just one press conference about racism. After meeting Mrs. Parks, he referred to her time and again, and he started speaking out frequently with conviction:

> "No one can deny that, today, the family of nations needs a concerted program of action to address Racism. We need to explore new ways to foster, for the future, the harmonious co-existence and interaction of individuals and peoples, in full respect of each other's dignity, identity, history and tradition. We need a culture in which we recognize, in every man and woman, a brother and a sister with whom we can together walk the path of solidarity and peace.
>
> "Our world needs to be reminded that humanity exists as a single human family, within which the concept of racial superiority has no place.
>
> "The answer must be a clear 'no.' The fight against racism is urgent. It must be explicit and direct. Too often in history, uncritical societies have stood by inactive as new signs of racism raised their head. If we are not alert, hatred and racial intolerance can reappear in any society, no matter how advanced it may consider itself." [14]
>
> Pope John Paul II
> Speaking Before the United Nations, 2002

In Mrs. Parks' personal estimation, neither of them was a great leader, but rather, they were both "moral leaders." And as such, they both were beacons of hope and love.

**The Journey Home**

On the plane ride back to Washington D.C. after the press conference, I mustered the courage to ask, "Mrs. Parks, why did you invite me to come with you to meet the Pope? Me, of all people, especially because I'm White. Mrs. Parks didn't respond right away.

She thought for a while, as she always did, and responded, "Oh, Dear, I did not know you are White."

I wrote a poem on the trip home, sitting next to her on the incredible journey that we had. I read this to her and she patted my hand and smiled, her eyes shining with purpose—and most of all, love..

*Trust*
*Personal integrity generates trust*
*and goes beyond honesty.*
*Honesty Is*
*conforming words into reality.*
*Integrity is*
*conforming character to reality.*

## State of the Union Address

On January 19, 1999, President Bill Clinton delivered the State of the Union Address. Brother Willis had been trying for days to simply get Mrs. Parks a ticket to the address. She was staying at The Mansion, and he felt it important that she be there.

He kept going to the White House and coming back to The Mansion, saying he would have to go again. This was at the time when issues associated with the president and Monica Lewinsky were reported by the press daily. White House aides were putting out fires everywhere. The day of the address, Willis told me it was a 50/50 chance whether Mrs. Parks would be invited.

I made a call to a good friend of the Clintons, Susan Thomases. She made one phone call and within a half hour, Hillary Clinton made a personal call to Mrs. Parks, inviting her to the address.

All of Congress was nervous. Everyone was afraid of the political fallout because of the scandal. President Clinton, a master at public speaking, had prepared a great speech. Any other year, Congress

Mrs. Parks stands as she is honored during President Clinton's State of the Union Address, Washington D.C., January 19, 1999. Beside her is Tipper Gore, Vice President Al Gore's wife, and Major League baseball player Sammy Sosa. (Photo: David Hume Kennerly/Getty Images)

would have been on its feet cheering. Instead, everyone sat, hands folded in their laps or around their chest, in deafening silence. That is, until President Clinton announced the guest who was seated next to Mrs. Clinton.

Everyone in the room stood, turned toward Mrs. Parks, and greeted her with a thunderous bipartisan ovation. The clapping and cheering were deafening and unending. It was as if all the dignitaries, legislators, and judges had reserved their applause for Mrs. Parks. It went on and on and on as if all of Congress, the Supreme Court judges, and other dignitaries didn't want to sit back down.

Later that night, I asked Mrs. Parks how she felt receiving an extended standing ovation from members of Congress and other dignitaries. I told her I was so proud of her and proud of that moment, one I will never forget.

Mrs. Parks' Congressional Gold Medal of Honor, given to her in 1999. (Photo: Library of Congress)

She didn't answer me right away, but when she did, she replied, "I was so honored to be able to help our great country."

I was stunned by her response. I am still stunned by the power of those words, her power. In her own words, she would have described it differently. She would say, "It is always, always, about God's work."

## The Presidential Medal of Freedom

Mrs. Rosa Parks was the recipient of numerous honors, awards, and accolades. In 1996, she was awarded the Presidential Medal of Freedom.

She appreciated each award she received, no matter how small or large, and she understood the importance of the recognitions to continue spreading her message. She wasn't one to bask in the limelight, but she stepped forward to bring attention to her mission, vision, and values.

Her honors were not ego opportunities for Mrs. Parks, but rather, were used as opportunities to be messengers for what is right.

Mrs. Parks displays her Congressional Gold Medal of Honor with Vice President Al Gore prior to a benefit tribute concert in her honor, November 28, 1999, in Detroit. (Photo: Getty Images/ Paul Sancya / Pool)

## The Congressional Medal of Honor

In 1999, Mrs. Rosa Parks was awarded the Congressional Medal of Honor, the country's highest civilian award. She truly deserved the honor but getting her this recognition took a lot of work lobbying Congress. We lobbied on Capitol Hill for many months with critical support and heavy lifting from the NAACP and the Congressional Black Caucus.

The campaign to honor Mrs. Parks began after she was assaulted in her Detroit home in 1994. At the time, she had no health insurance because she couldn't afford it. Brother Edwards had been surprised to learn that no health insurance came with this medal. He said he was embarrassed when he had to tell her she would not be insured like he was, as a Vietnam War veteran. Mr. Willis wept when he found out that Congress would not help pay for Mrs. Parks' health insurance. I don't think anyone in Congress could believe that she had no money, considering how famous she had become.

But sorrowful tears do not betray a lack of strength or character; quite the opposite. Brother Willis' tears expanded his horizons and gave him hope and a new mission—not just for her, but also for so many others who had devoted their lives to fighting for freedom on battlefields other than war. Even after she passed, he stayed with us to continue his fight to get those heroes health insurance.

Mrs. Parks' medal was designed by our artist-in-residence at the time, Artis Lane. Canadian born, she had emigrated to Detroit. Also, an activist, she and Mrs. Parks had been good friends for many years. Mrs. Lane even gave the O Museum in The Mansion the model she used to have the actual medal made. It is proudly displayed on the back of a secret door leading to her favorite room, the Gallery, where she hosted most of her gospel brunches and tea parties.

Ms. Anita Peek, executive director of the Rosa and Raymond Parks Institute, told a documentary filmmaker from Minnesota that Brother Willis and I were responsible for getting Mrs. Parks the Congressional

Medal of Honor. It was our idea, but giving us the credit still doesn't seem right. Mrs. Parks was responsible for her receiving this medal. She earned it and every accolade she ever received. We were simply instruments that facilitated this coming to fruition.

## Knowing the Difference

Initially, neither Mrs. Parks or I understood the difference between the Presidential Medal of Freedom and her Congressional Medal of Honor. But we were both so happy she received them and thankful that Mr. Willis had worked so hard in succeeding to get her these awards.

Mr. Willis explained to us that the primary difference between them is that the Presidential Medal of Freedom is personally awarded by the president of the United States, while Congressional Medals are awarded by acts of Congress. He also explained that the Presidential Medal is awarded for admirable contributions to the security or national interests of the United States—world peace, or cultural or other significant public or private endeavors. But a Congressional Medal is the highest honor a civilian can receive because one person doesn't make the decision regarding its recipients, but rather, all the congresspersons—who rarely agreed on anything.

Mrs. Parks and I giggled like young girls when he told us. We still both didn't quite understand the differences.

But I remember how deeply moved Mrs. Parks was by receiving them. Still, she firmly believed that others deserved these awards more than she.

ROTC cadets, Scouts, youth groups, and others accompany Mrs. Parks' body as she was transported to St. Paul AME Church in Montgomery in a horse-drawn carriage for public viewing on October 29, 2005 in Montgomery, Alabama. (Photo: Justin Sullivan/Getty Images)

## And Then, She Was Gone

Mrs. Parks traveled constantly. I did not always go with her, particularly when she traveled to Detroit, as she had so many people working at the Institute. However, she would always return.

Then one time, she didn't.

Sadly, I don't remember the last time she stayed with me, or what our last words were before she made her final journey to Detroit. Unfortunately, I have no notes in my journals about this.

Brother Willis was with me when we found out that Mother Parks had suffered a severe stroke. He was grief stricken, but he sprung to action to do what he could to help find caretakers for what turned out to be around the clock care.

I asked him if I should go to Detroit. He was firm. "No," he said. As always, he was thinking of others. A product of my upbringing, when men told us what we should do, we women of the 1950's did what we were told. He asked me not to tell anyone about her stroke. He stayed with me a few more weeks, and then flew back to Los Angeles, where he was based.

When Mrs. Parks passed on October 24, 2005, it did not come as a shock because I knew her frail state; nevertheless, when death creeps around you, especially when its someone you truly love, the news is unsettling.

Upon news of her death, Mr. Willis sprang into action, making all the arrangements for four grand funerals. I have never met anyone more loving and more capable of making his dreams for other people real. He was so much like Mrs. Parks for me—bigger than life itself. He made heaven on earth happen, for others.

Mr. Willis was the connector, the communicator. He was the true visionary, making Mrs. Parks' dreams—and all those around her—real, even in death.

*"Try to remember that death is as natural as living. God uses us all."*

*~ Mrs. Rosa Parks*

# Mrs. Parks' Four Funerals

My family and I accompanied Mrs. Parks' body to the funeral locations. Each of our children took one leg of the journey. It was a fitting way for us to bid farewell to this wonderful lady. But, when you know truly special people, like Mr. Willis and Mrs. Parks, you never truly bid them farewell. They are in your heart, mind, and conversations daily.

### *Montgomery*

Mrs. Rosa Parks passed away in her Detroit apartment on October 24, 2005, fittingly on the exact date that the United Nations was founded, October 24, 1945. Her body lay in state at the Capitol Rotunda in Washington D.C. She was the first woman ever given this honor, as well as the first African American. Even in death she continued to break barriers.

I was a pallbearer at her funeral services in Montgomery, Washington D.C., and Detroit. Brother Willis worked with Karen Price-Ward to get Southwest Airlines to donate an airplane and crew for transporting Mrs. Parks' casket to each city. The pilot, Captain Lou Freeman, was the first African-American chief pilot for a commercial airline in US history.

In Montgomery, the service was held at St. Paul African Methodist Episcopal Church, which has a quaint, beautiful sanctuary. It was my favorite memorial service of the three because I knew how much Mrs. Parks loved Montgomery—and she loved keeping things simple. Brother Willis was responsible for all logistics. Mrs. Parks had requested a simple service at her church, and he created exactly what she envisioned. It was a humble, beautiful service.

Her close friends from childhood came. Only one politician was there, Secretary of State Condoleezza Rice. Mr. Willis didn't want politics brought into this service because that is not what Mrs. Parks would have wanted. But the secretary insisted, saying she also is from

Montgomery. As she got to the pulpit and started to speak, people in the audience started to boo. It was uncomfortable and disrespectful and something Mrs. Parks would not have liked at all.

After the service, my husband, my son, and I walked with everyone to a reception at Mrs. Parks' museum at Troy State University, located not far from the church. There I talked with Rev. Jesse Jackson, Sr. and Rev. Al Sharpton at length. I talked with some of the board members and staff from Mrs. Parks' museum at the university, as I had been on the founding board.

But I also remember that right across the street was Mrs. Parks' favorite hat shop, still open, from the days before she moved to Detroit. Every time Mrs. Parks, Elaine, and I were in Alabama (and it was many times), we made a visit to the shop part of our itinerary. I always bought hats for everyone. It was always such great fun.

Elaine, my husband, and I left the reception and went to the hat shop. As always, there must have been over 2,000 church hats on display, in all shapes and sizes. I bought Elaine a wonderful hat. The shop now carried shoes, so in Mrs. Parks' honor, I also bought her a fun pair that matched her hat. Mrs. Parks would have enjoyed that had she been with us.

The wow moment came when we were leaving Montgomery and Captain Freeman tipped the wing of our airplane down toward the city. Many of us got teary. His voice over the speaker of the plane was cracking with emotion as he told us about his life as the first African-American captain, giving many thanks to the icon whose remains he was flying. It was such a fitting gesture toward Mrs. Parks. No one on the plane spoke for a very long time; we were all absorbed and lost in the moment.

### Washington D.C.'s Two Funerals

The second funeral service in Washington, D.C. was held at the Metropolitan African Methodist Episcopal Church, located very close to The Mansion and O Museum. Just before the service, Brother Willis

President George W. Bush, First Lady Laura Bush, and members of the US House and Senate attend a ceremony for Mrs. Parks in the Capitol Rotunda, October 30, 2005, in Washington, D.C. Mrs. Parks lying in state was a rare tribute for a private citizen and the first such honor for a woman. (Photo: Andrew Councill/AFP via Getty Images)

ran into the Amnesia Room where my husband, Ted, and I were sitting and listening to music. "We're late! We have to get to the church right away." Ted replied, "But Mr. Willis, you aren't wearing a suit." I will never forget the surprise on Brother Willis' face when he looked down and realized he was wearing jeans and a t-shirt.

Focused on orchestrating Mrs. Parks' memorial service, he hadn't paid attention to himself. He said, "Oh, I don't have a suit." Ted said, "When is the last moment we have to be in the church?"

Brother Willis said, "Twenty minutes, max."

Ted got his shirt, shoe, and suit size and said, "I'll meet you at the church."

Ted raced to Brooks Brothers, then to the church. He pulled Brother Willis into a bathroom to get properly dressed. It's amazing how quickly you can accomplish something, when given a purpose and a timeline.

Willis, who never had money himself, was just like Mrs. Parks—selfless, only thinking of others. He was very appreciative of the gesture.

Mrs. Parks' third funeral was a service at the Rotunda for political dignitaries. First, her body lay in state. Thirty thousand people came to thank her and pay her tribute. I was standing next to President George H. W. Bush when Brother Willis ran up to us. President Bush said, "I know you. You are the guy who always makes things happen."

That was so true. Brother Willis was always in the right place, doing the right thing. He was the best advance man ever. He knew exactly what to do, always.

### Detroit

After Washington, we flew to Detroit for the final ceremonies and burial. Mrs. Parks lay in repose at the Charles H. Wright Museum of African American History. It was a solemn and dignified setting.

Below: A group of mourners hold a tribute to civil rights pioneer Rosa Parks while waiting to catch a glimpse of the horse-drawn casson that carried her body to the Greater Grace Temple in Detroit in 2005. (Photo by Bill Pugliano/Getty Images)

Above: Detroit police officer Levan Adams watches a hearse carrying the casket of Mrs. Parks leaving Detroit's Charles H. Wright Museum of African American History on Wednesday, November 2, 2005. Viewing was held at the museum until 5:00 a.m. The procession carried Mrs. Parks to the Greater Grace Temple, where the funeral was held. (Photo: Bryan Mitchell/Getty Images)

Below: Mourners examine the bus made famous by Mrs. Parks at the Charles H. Wright Museum of African-American History in Detroit, where Mrs. Parks lay in repose in 2005. (Photo: Bill Pugliano/Getty Images)

The museum has a lot of history with Mrs. Parks and was a fitting place for her remains to lie. Her funeral service was held on November 2, 2005, at the Greater Grace Temple Church in Detroit.

Brother Willis arranged everything. He was more than upset that the dignitaries talked longer than their allotted time. He kept on mumbling under his breath, "This service was only supposed to take three hours." He was also surprised that more people got up to speak than had been scheduled. But he did not interrupt anyone. He ensured that small children were rotated through the service, up front, and in the laps of dignitaries. He made sure they had their pictures taken with all the famous people. He kept saying, "Mrs. Parks would want this," and he was so right.

This service lasted seven and a half hours.

My favorite speech was given at her last funeral by a then little-known senator from Illinois, Barack Obama. His words were simple, yet prophetic: "The woman we honored today held no public office, she wasn't a wealthy woman, didn't appear in the society pages. And yet when the history of this country is written, it is this small, quiet woman whose name will be remembered long after the names of senators and presidents have been forgotten."

The most memorable, surprising event at the funeral was Aretha Franklin. She was supposed to sing only one song, but when Reverend Jesse Jackson got up to speak, she was on the dais. She was so moved by his words that she started singing "I'll Fly Away." Tears of joy were streaming down my face and so many others. To witness the magic of love coming out of Aretha's soul was a once-in-a-lifetime opportunity. O Street Museum in The Mansion recorded a video, with permission from Ms. Franklin's estate and from Rev. Jackson, of the two of them in that moment. Watch and you will feel the power of the moment also.

So many of the dignitaries who spoke were not on the program, including Senator Obama, but I was so glad Brother Willis gave them all a chance to speak. I remembered how many times Mrs. Parks wanted to speak and wasn't given the chance. Letting everyone speak that wanted to was karmic and a fitting tribute to her.

We missed our earlier flight back to Washington D.C. because the funeral went so long. We were standing in the cold around 10 p.m., on a very cold and windy Detroit winter night. The horse with the carriage that had carried her casket was next to us. Brother Willis said, "There are no hotel rooms left in Detroit. I got you a special flight to D.C. at no cost. You will miss your flight if you don't leave now. You see that car over there. It is waiting to take you to the airport."

We gave him a big hug, thanking him for remembering us, especially as he was juggling everyone and everything. We walked over to the car he pointed to, not realizing that it was a police car. The policeman who drove us to the airport used his siren. We got to the airport just in time for our flight.

ARETHA FRANKLIN
& REV. JESSE JACKSON
~ "I'LL FLY AWAY"

Singer Aretha Franklin with Rev. Jesse Jackson in 2005 at Mrs. Parks' Detroit memorial service. (Photo by Paul Warner/WireImage, Getty Images)

"Brother" Willis Edwards was featured in a 2002 *Los Angeles Times* article, where he was dubbed, "The Fixer" because of his behind-the-scenes involvement in making things happen and getting things done. (Photo by Clarence Williams/*Los Angeles Times* via Getty Images)

# THE FIXER

Born in Texas in 1946, Edwards was drafted by the military, wounded in a land mine explosion during the Vietnam War, and was awarded a Bronze Star. He was well known in local and national circles as a "fixer" who worked on many elections, including the presidential campaign of Senator Robert F. Kennedy. Indeed, Edwards was by his side when the senator was assassinated.

While on the NAACP board, he headed the Hollywood Branch and sued *The Arsenio Hall Show* for discrimination. (Hall employed more than two hundred people, and none were African American). All the lawsuit proceeds went to the NAACP. He then helped create the

NAACP Image Awards, which he produced with Roone Arledge at ABC for two years. Every cent of the money he received from ABC went to the NAACP.

As he struggled to recover from an AIDS-related illness in 1984, Brother Willis was visited by Mrs. Parks. She compelled him, as he lay dying in the hospital, to get well—to help her, as she had no medical insurance to pay her bills. Five days later he left the hospital with a mission to serve her for the rest of her life.

We always called him Brother Willis or Mr. Willis. He created "The Street Committee on O Street," and every day we would spend at least an hour outside, sitting on the stoop, talking with everyone who walked by and asking them to sign our petitions. He would joke with Mrs. Parks that creating the Street Committee was a great way to show the five neighbors on the street who didn't like Black people that we were not afraid of them.

One story about Mr. Willis and his love for Mrs. Parks still haunts me. Just before my husband and I got into the police car to go to the Detroit airport after Mrs. Parks' funeral Mr. Willis bowed his head and said, "I will die now. I have no purpose to live anymore."

We were stunned. Neither of us knew what to say, so I simply hugged him for a long time, not wanting to let go and whispered, "I need you. Mr. Willis. I love you."

A week later he was staying with us again—thank goodness—and he got a call from his sister. She was at the courthouse. She had been issued a prison sentence. Could he please come back to Los Angeles to care for her two children until she got out of jail? He was on a plane to LA three hours later. That call gave him seven more years of life. Six months after his sister was released from prison, he passed away.

When he stayed with us, he taught us so much about humility and service to others. Brother Willis served on our museum board from 1995–2012, when he departed this life to serve God in heaven. Not one day goes by without stories and thoughts about Mr. Willis, our chosen brother.

## Mrs. Parks' Safehouse

My neighbors across the street had called the police during Mrs. Parks' birthday celebration. Well in 2008, they moved to California, and just as Mrs. Parks predicted I bought their house (this time not with credit card cash advances, but with my whole life insurance policy). And that is how The Rosa Parks Safehouse came to be.

Our own artist-in-residence and Mrs. Parks' close friend, Artis Lane, painted a beautiful picture depicting Mrs. Parks in that iconic moment on the bus. She titled it, *The Beginning*. One of the original limited-edition lithographs, signed by Mrs. Parks, hangs in the Safehouse, as Brother Willis gave it to us.

At 7:00 a.m., December 5, 2008, we dedicated 2015 O Street to Mrs. Parks, and have been calling it The Rosa Parks Safehouse ever since. Two days before, Brother Willis said, "Do you have a big pair of scissors? Do you have a red carpet?" Of course, I didn't. Thank goodness he reminded me so we could rush out and get these things.

Brother Willis and Mrs. Steele were there for the dedication. It was a blessed and forgiving day. After the dedication, we went to the main house for a lovely prayer breakfast.

## Advisor to Young and Old

When Anita Peek's son was nineteen, he wanted to adopt an African name, Adisa Foluke. He chose it very carefully: Adisa means "one who is clear" and Foluke means "the redeemer" or "the one who distinguishes between right and wrong." He was afraid to tell his mother and his grandmother that he wanted to change his name because he feared both would be very upset.

His mother later confirmed, "And rightfully so."

He went to Mrs. Parks and told her why it was important to him, asking for her help. She said to him gently, "This is wonderful. What a beautiful name you have given yourself."

And then, at just the right moment, while having dinner with Anita, her sister Elaine, and Anita's mother, Mother Parks said, "Your son (nodding toward Anita) and your grandson (nodding toward Anita's mother) loves you deeply. He is afraid to tell you he wants to change his name because he doesn't want to dishonor you, but it is important to him. His is old enough to change his name on his own. If this is what he wants, you should honor his desire."

And so, he changed his name legally, with their blessing, and everyone honored him. Right after this he became active in Mrs. Parks' Pathways to Freedom program, which traces the Underground Railroad into the Civil Rights Movement and beyond. It is supported by extended curriculum components implemented throughout the year within local communities. He worked there for many years, side-by-side with his mother, Elaine, and Mrs. Parks. His passion was this program.

Mrs. Parks used to be on the bus with all the children, but in the last few years of her life, the bus would come to her, to hear her first-hand stories. She was waiting for them at The Mansion and O Museum on July 29, 1997, when we got the horrific word. On the way to D.C. from Virginia, the driver fell asleep at the wheel and the bus crashed, landing in a river. Adisa was the only one who perished. Two other children were injured in the accident.

Anita said to me that if it weren't for the "ropes" training course that her son had taught the children on this trip, more children would have drowned, and how proud she was of her son taking care of others first.

It was a very sad time for all. Darkness fell upon everyone. Anita was so glad no one else was hurt and so thankful for Mrs. Parks' guidance and love. Nothing ever stays the same, no matter how hard we try. It's not what you've lost, it's what you have found.

Mrs. Parks and Rev. Jane Gunter were reunited in 1992, thirty-seven years after their famous bus ride in Montgomery on December 1, 1955. (Photo: Library of Congress: 15045, No. 228)

## The People Important to Mrs. Parks

I had the privilege of meeting an amazing number of famous people—leaders of countries, respected actors, producers, entertainers, business leaders, directors, and artists—while living and traveling with Mrs. Parks.

The director, producers, and actors in the movie, *The Rosa Parks Story*, starring Cecily Tyson and Angela Bassett, all met with Mrs. Parks here at O Museum in The Mansion to talk about this production. The original script, signed by those involved, is in our museum.

Through all this heady "stuff," Mrs. Parks never allowed it to affect her. She never lost sight of what was important, seizing each moment to pass the torch to other people to go forth, serving others with love, compassion, and hope.

Given the chance to talk to the president of the United States, of course, she would always say yes. When she visited, she would always carve out time to meet the Secret Service agents and the butlers.

That day in 1955, a young woman named Jane Gunter was on the Cleveland Street bus with Mrs. Parks, sitting right behind the driver. She was White, pregnant, and in her late teens, I believe. Her husband was stationed at the Maxwell Air Force Base in Montgomery, where she was on her way to meet him. Not knowing "the silent dog whistle rules of color," when Mrs. Parks was told to give up her seat, Mrs. Gunter offered her seat to the passenger rather than have Mrs. Parks move to the back of the bus.

A White man who was standing in front of her, holding onto the pole, blocked her with his knees and said, "Don't you dare move," in a sinister, angry tone that the young woman could not ignore. Another person, seated next to Mrs. Gunter, said, "You had better not move." She thought they might hurt her if she did, so she froze.

It wasn't until much later that she found out the person to whom she had offered her seat was Mrs. Rosa Parks. She wrote a letter to Mrs. Parks and asked for forgiveness for not believing she could stand up to help her.

Jane Gunter and Mrs. Parks became great friends—and pen pals! Mrs. Parks became the godmother of Mrs. Gunter's grandchildren. Thirty-seven years after their fateful bus ride together, they were reunited in Atlanta, where Mrs. Gunter then lived. "You were there," Mrs. Parks confirmed. Each had recently published a book, and each author signed copies of her book for the other.

Mrs. Parks was delighted to learn that Jane Gunter was a missionary, had become a pastor, and had founded Family Life Ministries, devoting countless hours each week giving civil right talks to students and parishioners. She looked forward to these letters and talked about them every time she got one of Reverend Gunter's handwritten letters. You never know who you will inspire. After Mrs. Parks passed, nearly every year the Reverend and her beautiful daughter, Jan, would come to The Mansion on Mrs. Parks' February 4 birthday, to commemorate her friendship and share stories with others about Mrs. Parks.

She was also invited by the Library of Congress—which is a big deal—to be front and center on the stage at their opening of "Mrs. Rosa Parks: Her Story." December 5, 2019, My husband and I were there to watch and listen to her. Here was a woman who made a simple gesture of kindness, being publicly rewarded. "It's never about the big things," Mrs. Parks would say. "It's about taking risks, opening your heart, doing the right thing."

Mrs. Parks gave Reverend Gunter a dress she was wearing while teaching one of her computer classes in Detroit. It is pure karma that this dress was given to her by Mrs. Parks and that she since donated the dress to The O Museum.

We each have our own way, our own mode of survival, our own path to salvation, our own view of our mission, our own notion on religion, our own, unique fingerprints, our own choice of how we respond to the cards we are dealt. No one is wrong.

Direct kindness and kind direction are possible. Every breath we take is a gift. Little things add up to big things.

Love begets love.

## Going to Church with Mrs. Parks

Going to church was one of Mrs. Parks' favorite activities. Until the last year of her life, she never missed a Sunday service unless she was in the hospital. On the days when she was too ill to leave her bed, she had a preacher and friends come say prayers with her.

Getting ready for church gave her pleasure, too. She loved having her hair just right and choosing just the right outfit, including the purse, shoes, jewelry, and dress. And, of course, just the right hat. She always smiled, from the moment she got up on Sunday morning until the service started. At that very moment, she lost herself in God.

She greeted everyone, whether she knew them or not. Her eyes shined with purpose. When we went to church without Bro. Willis Edwards, people did not know we were coming. She would guide us to where she wanted us to sit—in the back, off to the side, so we would not take anyone else's seat. She would say, "We don't want to get un-Christian looks when we sit in someone else's place." No matter how many times I heard her say that, I always smiled.

But every time we would sit down, no matter at what church, someone would come up to her and whisper in her ear that she should move to the front. She would always respond that we all would need to move with her, which would take up someone else's place, which she did not want to do. Sometimes we would move, sometimes we wouldn't.

When Brother Edwards was with us, he always advanced our visit. The elders of the church would greet us outside and guide us to the VIP area. They would always be amazed at those times when we pulled up to the front of the church in my little yellow school bus. They expected a limousine. Mrs. Parks was always embarrassed to be treated differently than anyone else. Still, she told me she was glad I didn't have to look for a parking space for my yellow bus and could go right into church with her. No one ever tickets a yellow school bus!

What remained constant in all the worship services we attended over the years was that the moment the preacher started to speak she would lose herself in the service.

Nothing else existed, except for the Word of the Lord. Every Sunday, she lost herself in God. It was an amazing thing to accompany her to these services and be in the presence of such a truly blessed woman.

## The Library of Congress Collection and Exhibition

Twenty years before Mrs. Parks passed away, she wrote a will giving her estate and all her intellectual property to the one place she was passionate about—the organization she created to honor her beloved husband and help defenseless children—The Rosa and Raymond Parks Institute for Self-Development (RRPI).

When she died, her will was contested by her nephews and nieces, who thought that she was wealthy. Far from it! But while she didn't have much money, she did have an amazing collection of letters, books, and documents about her life. Not just as the mother of the Civil Rights Movement, but also of her years working for women's rights and children's rights. There were letters from Dr. Martin Luther King, Jr., books signed by Malcolm X, and awards aplenty. Perhaps most amazing was the collection of her copious notes of all the meetings she attended from the 1930s on.

All her personal effects were given to her best friend, the daughter she never birthed—and wanted to adopt—RRPI co-founder Elaine Steele. Ms. Steele was sued first, the apparent line of thinking being that if she had received all the personal effects, she also must have gotten her money as well. When they found out that Mrs. Parks had no money, they sued RRPI.

Initially, the courts ruled against her will and in favor of a court trustee taking over her estate. This was against Mrs. Parks' wishes. When RRPI lost in the first round, the courts supposedly gave everything to Guernsey's auction house to organize and prepare for sale.

To stop this, an injunction was placed on the sale of her personal effects to prevent the sale of Mrs. Parks' items piece by piece. RRPI wanted her things returned because that was Mrs. Parks' passion. The organization was not interested in how much money they were sold for, but rather that they be returned. The courts awarded Elaine one half of a vote and her sister, Anita, another half of a vote. The court's receivership gave themselves one vote, and the "family" of Mrs. Parks (her nephews and nieces) one vote. That meant it was always two-to-one against Mrs. Parks' wishes.

The court of Wayne County in Detroit then gave notice to RRPI that it had thirty days to pick up their personal things. Only this did not happen because the day after the order, the courts sent agents to move everything out, thinking RRPI might remove important pieces.

But just the opposite occurred. Many of the pieces of Mrs. Parks' life and legacy disappeared mysteriously.

Before the courts reversed their opinion in the higher courts of Michigan, Howard Buffett (son of billionaire investor Warren Buffett) bought everything for the sum everyone involved had agreed upon. Remember, RRPI didn't necessarily agree, but it only had one vote and the two votes superseded theirs.

Howard Buffett (God bless him!) knew how important her papers were to the world. He donated the complete collection to the Library of Congress. But he didn't stop there. He donated money to the library to curate her collection of things no one had known about or seen. This was the chance to tell her story.

Anita and Elaine told me they had discussed the distribution of Mrs. Parks' personal property with her long before she passed. Never in her wildest imagination did she think her possessions were important enough to interest the Library of Congress (LOC).

They also told me that even if she had thought she was important enough, had she donated them to the LOC, her things probably would have stayed in containers because there had been no one to curate everything. Elaine and Anita agreed that Howard Buffet's donation to the LOC was the biggest blessing that had ever happened to them (other than the honor to get to serve Mrs. Parks' mission, of course).

Mrs. Parks would be so happy to know that the library has her collection and that it was being curated with such love and respect. In the truest sense of the word, the curatorial work the LOC has done for Mrs. Parks has been a godsend. Bless you, Howard Buffet, for your gift of Mrs. Parks' legacy to the LOC.

## Back to Detroit

In October 2019, I flew to Detroit, with my son, Z Stein, to read portions of this book to Ms. Anita Peek, executive director of RRPI and her sister Elaine, RRPI co-founder.

From the age of nine, Z's formative years were spent while Mrs. Parks lived here. She had made a big impact on him. As a lawyer, he knew it was important to make sure that the memories of my time with Mother Parks were accurate, and he wanted to share this time with me.

I was—and probably always will be—deeply affected by these meetings. The sisters gently corrected me when I wasn't completely accurate and added much insight to what I had witnessed. I was and remain very appreciative of the time they spent with us.

Detroit was very hot when we were there. We spent three days reading from my notes, getting their feedback, and driving around Detroit, learning more about the city.

Our first day there, we met at RRPI, which was located next door to Mrs. Parks' home. The house/office was filled with purpose but decaying like many parts of our inner cities. On the drive there from the downtown hotel where we were staying, we encountered blocks and blocks of roofs that were caving in, even on buildings near their home, with people still living inside.

When we arrived, Ms. Peek greeted us. A gentleman she was taking care of was also there. He was struggling to get up to leave the room where we would be meeting. When he left, the room smelled of sweat and illness. She always took care of others less fortunate than she.

Ms. Elaine Steele arrived moments later, and we hugged. I was happy to be with them again. We then all sat down for what turned out to be the first of several six-and-a half hour meetings, as I read so many of these pages. None of us knew beforehand that it would last this long. No one ate or drank anything during these meetings. We were all so absorbed in what I had written about Mrs. Parks that nothing else existed.

Mrs. Parks shows off the Wonder Woman Foundation's special 1984 Eleanor Roosevelt Woman of Courage Award presented to her on November 14, 1984. At left is actress Cicely Tyson, who presented the award. (Photo: Bettman via Getty Images)

There was no air-conditioning in the room either. It was uncomfortable at first because it was so hot outside. But once we started talking about Mrs. Parks, the heat no longer mattered. Nothing mattered but sharing our collective stories.

I read them my stories. They said, "Amen," to much of it. These two women are so committed to Mother Parks' legacy. When they questioned something that they had forgotten, or wasn't sure if I should disclose, I would point to Mrs. Parks' books where Mrs. Parks had written down her memories. And they would say, "Okay."

We also spent time talking off the record about how difficult it has been for the sisters after Mrs. Parks' death.

From their perspective, they watched through the years as others have profited and used Mrs. Parks to raise money for themselves. They had watched silently, sharing her pain, when Mrs. Parks endured being invited to speak, only to have other dignitaries take over her time.

They were not part of the famous Selma March, but Mrs. Parks told them many times what it was like when she walked those long eight miles, being told, "Get to the side of the road. You should not be here." But others who knew her importance invited her back in.

Mrs. Parks finished all eight miles of the Selma March, quietly ignoring the indignity of this treatment. At the end of the march, the press, seeing her at the back of the line, stopped the line to bring her to the front for the photo opp. Years later, when the movie about Selma was being made, they told me Mrs. Parks was not in the movie, even though it was produced and directed by a woman.

Life is filled with many curve balls and irregular turns.

Mrs. Rosa Parks is a true hero, who suffered like a saint. But still, time after time, she continued to take the high road, never complaining, just putting one foot in front of the other. That is who she was.

At these meetings, I learned that during the last year of Mrs. Parks' life, when she was bedridden and totally infirmed after having suffered a major stroke, Elaine and Anita refused to send her to a nursing home. They wanted her to stay with them, even though she didn't know where she was, or even that she was infirmed.

Lois Harris, actress Cicely Tyson's assistant (and a true saint), moved in to care for Mrs. Parks around the clock in Detroit. I remember at dinner after the funeral in Montgomery, Alabama, when Brother Willis told me with such pride that she was so well-taken care of "that she didn't have a bruise on her body from being bedridden so long." Miss Lois told me how wonderful the time was that she spent with her, and what an honor it was to take care of Mother Parks, and that her favorite thing was to hold her hand and talk with her.

Questions abound. Why is it that so many have profited from Mrs. Parks, but her caretakers live day-to-day with such limited funds? Could it be because they are women? Could it be because they are not entrepreneurs? Why would the courts allow Mrs. Parks' last will and testament to be questioned?

Does it matter when it was Mrs. Parks who trusted them? I think so. It matters greatly that these two ladies suffered because they fought for Mrs. Parks' wishes. Like Mrs. Parks, they would not take "No" for an answer.

Mrs. Parks had something big to say. Bigger than just the bus boycott. Yet except for her books and letters, very few people gave her the opportunity. She knew, years before others did, that her will would be contested, but she could do nothing to stop it. She even did a videotape to prove that she was of sound mind.

Life is too short to live in the shadows. Truth is relentless. The saving grace is empathy.

### Revisiting Detroit Two Years Later

Is it easy to understand, but hard to explain? Or is it easy to explain then hard to understand?

It had been years since I had been in Mrs. Parks' Detroit home at 9336 Wildemere Street. In March 2021, my husband and I visited the sisters again. They asked if we wanted to see Mrs. Parks' home again, where "it" happened. I was a little surprised by being asked, but we agreed to go.

Her house was now stuffed and piled up high, nearly touching the ceiling, with the historical papers, artifacts, and clothes.

When Ms. Anita Peek, whose offices are next door to Mrs. Parks' house, walked us through the house, she showed us where her kitchen had been torn out by a contractor who never came back to finish the job. You could see the lathes that once held up the plaster walls, as well as holes in the walls exposing the interior to the harsh weather of Detroit.

What motivated them to want to modernize this kitchen after her death is beyond me. It would have been more important to bring tours to see how Mrs. Parks lived, with her authentic kitchen. So many people would have loved this.

There were so many papers and boxes, as if they were holding up the roof. So much of the pain that she had described about her life, the

Below: Elaine Steele, H.H. Leonards, and Anita Peek in 2021, standing outside Mrs. Parks' Detroit home (right) where she was assaulted, and the Rosa and Raymond Parks Institute (left). (Photo: Ted Spero, O Museum at The Mansion on O Street)

"assault" (as she referred to the rape) that occurred there, and the stories of what happened after she passed, made it difficult for me to breathe.

Ms. Peek also pointed out where the attack had happened on the narrow stairs leading to the second floor. We couldn't walk up the stairs because they were filled with boxes of Mrs. Parks' possessions. But I didn't want to go up, even if the boxes were not blocking our path. I was shivering from the realization that this is where Mrs. Parks was badly beaten and assaulted. The shock of her home in such disrepair was overwhelming.

I was so upset that Mrs. Parks' meticulously cataloged papers were being destroyed, left unprotected from the elements of the outside world (although a few had cut-open plastic garbage bags duct taped over them where the ceiling was stained and crumbling from water damage) that I thought I was going to pass out, as I had when my racist neighbor put those rats in my face. It was as if the walls and roof were leaking tears from heaven.

My husband recognized that I was close to fainting. Without even asking me, he took my arm and gently guided me outside. He told me later that he was angered by what he saw. I had no strength in me and was so grateful he took charge. We drove away shortly after that, shaking our heads in disbelief. He is still angry, and I remain simply heartbroken.

I often recount Mrs. Parks saying, "You have to take the first step." She would tell me, "Don't be afraid. You will fail if you don't take that step." What was most remarkable was observing Mrs. Parks consciously choose to become stronger from adversity. Each time something bad happened, she chose to live with greater purpose.

Her legacy needs to be protected.

## Change Has to Come

Mrs. Parks was a warrior, but she felt sad about not being allowed to speak openly more often about what she believed in. She was a warrior. Still, she never complained about how she was treated.

Mrs. Parks always said that we have a choice on who we want to become. In her own words: "Human beings are set apart from the animals. We have a spiritual self, a physical self, and a conscience."

We can make choices and we are responsible for the choices we make. Mrs. Parks knew this, preached it, and lived it. She never sought the limelight she lived in for much of her life. She was a woman of great faith. She understood the spirituality of humility.

Mrs. Parks resolved that, "When I die, I want to be stronger than when I started." She knew that it would be a tragedy to get old and then compromise what she had lived for. This is why when she healed her spirit and body after her horrific assault in her Detroit home, she became stronger and more resolved to help her human family.

Mrs. Parks loved children. This photo was taken with a group of children at a restaurant (between 1980 and 1990) and is one of many such photographs in the Rosa Parks collection at the Library of Congress. (Photo: Library of Congress, 2015648558)

# WHAT IS YOUR STORY?

If you have a story and/or photos of you and Mrs. Parks, please send them to us at rosaparks@omuseum.org, and we will post them on our website and/or in our next book! Help share her words today. Everyone needs to know her message of hope:

"As I grow older, I see that there is still so much work to do. I want to share the message of peace and justice for all of humanity with the world. I am grateful to God for this long life. I am thankful that He has used me to fulfill some of His plans."

Mrs. Rosa Parks, *Dear Mrs. Parks: A Dialogue with Today's Youth*

## The Story Continues

On May 13, 2019, Washington D.C. Mayor Muriel Bowser dedicated a permanent plaque outside the O Museum in The Mansion, commemorating how Mrs. Parks made us her home-away-from-home and designating the building as an important historic site for the African American Heritage Trail. Around the same time, the Library of Congress asked us to partner on her exhibition and help with a year of programming.

Mrs. Parks' story, legacy, and connection to our city is little known, and yet critical to the work she did. With the #MeToo movement in full force and the racial tensions currently plaguing our country, her story is even more germane.

Still, with all her accolades, until I started writing about Mrs. Rosa Parks, I never quite understood how much she influenced and changed the trajectory of my life. A woman of few words, Mrs. Parks' actions forever impacted the lives of people all over the globe. Sometimes the important things in life start with putting one foot in front of the other—and then taking that big leap.

Mrs. Parks is a role model for many and for a variety of reasons. She quietly lived an exemplary life, teaching all of us who knew her that as complicated as we think the world is—and our lives are—it doesn't have to be that way. She lived the truth.

If we allow life to be simple, then her message will not simply be understood, but also embraced. In her own words: *"Each person must live as a model for others."* Mrs. Parks lived with purpose in every breath she took. She believed our actions are more important than our words. She lived her words.

## Disciples Never Die

Many people say God's name and praise God's name, but few are willing to be God's disciple. Mrs. Rosa Parks was one of the few who are willing to be a disciple. This is why we revere her, why we heed her profoundly wise words, and why we strive to keep her legacy alive.

Jesus said (Matthew 16:24) that any person who desires to be a disciple must do three things: (1) deny self; (2) pick up the cross (burden) for others; and (3) follow His example.

So few people are willing to deny themselves comfort, pleasure, or security for the sake of helping others. They instead choose a seat at the table of privilege, acceptability, or even mediocrity.

But not Mother Parks. Repeatedly throughout her long, blessed life, she denied herself comfort and accolades so she could serve others. She denied herself what most people are afraid to refuse—everything that threatens their security—for her mission and for human dignity.

Mrs. Parks didn't just deny herself; she knowingly and willingly picked up her cross. Hers was not the cross people wear dangling from an ear or adorned around their neck (although she did wear a beautiful cross many times). She took up the true cross, the heavy albatross that is sometimes inconvenient, painful, and burdensome. She carried the cross that brings rejection from most of society, but one that is essential to serving those in need.

Despite her living in an age when women were not supposed to be at the forefront, she triggered a movement, and remains the beam of light calling us to selfless action. She did it when she triggered the Civil Rights Movement with her act of defiance, and she sparked the genesis of the #MeToo movement when she began documenting African-American rape victims in the South during the 1930's.

Mrs. Parks practiced her faith within the African Methodist Episcopal Church, but for her being a disciple didn't carry a label like Christian, Muslim, Hindu, Jewish, or Buddhist. She believed these designations only serve to separate the family of God. She had many close friends from various religions, races, cultures, and ethnicities. She did not just tolerate other religious beliefs and customs, she went to their ashram, their church, their synagogue, their temple, and their mosque, and studied alongside them to learn what they believed.

She accepted all, loved all, and learned from all.

A disciple acts on principles—like denying oneself for the good of others. This allows us to focus on something bigger than self. Like Peter, who gave up his net to follow the way of Jesus and the Lord made him a fisher of humanity.

Mrs. Parks held a strong resolution, "When I die, I want to be stronger than when I started." She knew it would be a tragedy to grow old only to compromise what she had lived for. That is why at age 81, after she healed her spirit and body from the horrific attack in her Detroit home, she became stronger and more devoted to helping the family of humanity.

Since I met her not long after she was assaulted, I was blessed to be an eyewitness to this beautiful octogenarian growing stronger and more resilient despite her past traumas.

My sister, my mother, and the mother of many movements for human dignity sat down so that we might stand. She was a disciple who took up the cross against injustice.

We who call ourselves disciples today cannot honor her legacy simply through song and speech. Discipleship calls for action.

Her name will not die, and more importantly, the sacrifice she invested in humanity will never pass away. The spirit of the great disciple Rosa McCauley Parks can ever die as long as we follow her example to put aside self and extend ourselves for the benefit of humanity.

*Dedicated to Gary Tobin, the man behind this journey.*

Mrs. Parks and H. H. Leonards holding hands, as they frequently did. (Photo: O Street Museum in The Mansion)

## About the Author (In Her Own Words)

Many people have asked how I established The Mansion and O Museum, especially because I started with no money, no business background, and no art or design background. It started simply with a childlike openness to the visions God passed through me.

My first job in Washington D.C. was as a nanny for seven children. Seeing our nation's capital through the eyes of these children was wonderful, enlightening, and life changing. I have loved all my various jobs—working at a girls' reformatory, as a hospital assistant (a nice way to say bedpan cleaner), as a dishwasher, mental hospital caretaker, waitress, short-order cook, secretary, and working with severely handicapped children. Every job has contributed to my ability to balance vision with practical ways to get things done.

When I had the vision to create The Mansion—much like my friend and mentor, Mrs. Rosa Parks would do—I abandoned all outside influences and focused solely on the steady heart work of seeking God, one day and one night at a time. Each day over these more than forty years, I forgive everyone of everything; and each morning, I forgive myself.

With this philosophy as our cornerstone, The O Museum in The Mansion has become a way of life, not a business. We are a small, private luxury hotel and club, conference center, and event experience. Most important, we are a museum that has as its mission to empower people to do what they love—dare to be different—and have fun. We inspire creativity, diversity, and imagination through the fusion of the arts, science, and sports.

The creative process comes in many forms: from the wrinkles on our grandmother's face to a refugee's smile in Darfur. We combine art, architecture, literature, and inspiration to craft experiences. We have been a haven for heads of state, foreign dignitaries, business leaders, writers, artists, musicians, scientists, and prominent entertainers.

I am also a romantic, having opened our doors on Valentine's Day 1980. Within our walls and between them (but that's another story) novels, songs, paintings, and even legislation have been created.

While my proudest moments are the birth of my son, Z, and my marriage to Ted Spero, over the past four decades, many honors and blessings have come into my life. Having Mrs. Rosa Parks grace my life as a confidante and friend has been a true blessing. I met Pope John Paul with my adopted mother, Mrs. Parks. I've met with presidents and have had the good fortune to create iconic branding campaigns for multi-national corporations. I was commissioned to redesign and serve as general contractor on the first I. M. Pei building in Washington D.C. I proudly wrote the first $1 million check to the Statue of Liberty restoration campaign on behalf of American Express.

Mrs. Parks celebrating the Christmas holiday season with friends at The Mansion (Photo: O Street Museum in The Mansion)

Mrs. Parks with Z Stein (left), H. H. Leonards' son, and visiting friend Saw Lwin at The Mansion (Photo: O Street Museum in The Mansion)

I was privileged to be asked by the Rock 'n Roll Hall of Fame Museum to raise $500,000 for a major exhibit to commemorate John Lennon's sixtieth birthday (and the twentieth anniversary of his passing). Three days later, I was able to obtain a commitment letter from one corporation for twice that amount, plus another $500,000 worth of networking equipment.

Despite these accomplishments, many people may be surprised to know that I nearly flunked out of grade school and graduated from high school in the bottom ten of my class. As a result, at The Mansion we never look at anyone's resume; everyone has a clean slate and gets an equal opportunity to work and thrive.

Although I conceived and created this place, The Mansion and O Museum magic go well beyond me and will survive long after me. While I live and work here, most people don't know who I am—though I might valet their car, serve their meal, or bus their table after dinner.

My measure of "wealth" are my children Z Stein, Sonny, and Hannah, along with what we give back.

I am a testament to the fact that a person in America can start a dream without money, achieve a vision, and share a wealth that transcends a monetary figure. If we are true to our vision, committed to our path, and willing to share ourselves, we all can achieve things beyond what we know.

I still breathe because God has so many things for me to do. I still have many things to accomplish. Forty plus years is only a start.

I don't just believe in miracles; I rely on them. Magical moments in life really do exist.

H. H. Leonards, Founder
The Mansion and O Museum

# Endnotes

1. According to Danielle McGuire, author of *At the Dark End of the Street: Black Women, Rape, and Resistance* (Vintage, 2011), Mrs. Parks' investigation resulted in the formation of the Committee for Equal Justice, which later became known as the Montgomery Improvement Association. She writes, "the 1955 Montgomery bus boycott, often heralded as the opening scene of the civil rights movement, was in many ways the last act of a decades-long struggle to protect [B]lack women, like Taylor, from sexualized violence and rape" (McGuire, 2010; digital location 186).

   To quote the American Psychological Association (*apa.org*): "The social movement widely described as the Civil Rights Movement, emerged out of [B]lack women demanding control over their bodies and lives, [B]lack men being killed for protecting [B]lack women, or ultimately, the fight for [B]lack women's bodies and agency and against White supremacist rape and assault."

2. Emmett Till grew up on the southside of Chicago in the 1940's. On August 25, 1955, while visiting his uncle in Mississippi, he entered a store, purchased some candy and left. The woman at the counter alleged he grabbed her, made crude remarks, and wolf-whistled at her. Three days later her husband Roy Bryant and his brother-in-law J. W. Milam went to Emmett Till's uncle's house, where he was staying, and kidnapped him. Three days later his mutilated body was found in the Tallahatchie River. His mother, Mamie Till, chose to have an open casket funeral for her son to show everyone the horrors of what happened.

   The Reverend Jesse Jackson, a frequent guest of The Mansion said, "With his body water-soaked and defaced, most people would have kept the casket covered. His mother let the body be exposed. More than 100,000 people saw his body lying in that casket here in Chicago. That must have been, at that time, the largest single civil rights demonstration in American history."

   A month later on September 23, those involved were found not guilty after only an hour of jury deliberation. The tragedy of Emmett Till added fuel to the fire that was the beginning of the Civil Rights Movement.

3. "James Blake, 89; Driver Had Rosa Parks Arrested," by Jon Thurber. *Los Angeles Times*. March 26, 2002.

4. In 1909, Henry Moscowitz joined W. E. B. Du Bois and other civil rights leaders to establish the NAACP. Kivie Kaplan, a vice-chairman of the Union of American Hebrew Congregations (now the Union for Reform Judaism), served as the national president of the NAACP from 1966 to 1975. Arnie Aronson worked with A. Philip Randolph and Roy Wilkins to found the Leadership Conference.

   During the Civil Rights Movement, Jewish activists represented a disproportionate number of White people involved in the struggle. Jews made up half of the young people who participated in the Mississippi Freedom Summer in 1964. Leaders of the Reform Movement were arrested with Rev. Dr. Martin Luther King, Jr. in St. Augustine, Florida, in 1964 after a challenge to racial segregation in public accommodations. Most famously, Rabbi Abraham Joshua Heschel marched arm-in-arm with Dr. King during his 1965 March on Selma.

The Civil Rights Act of 1964 and the Voting Rights Act of 1965 were drafted in the conference room of Religious Action Center of Reform Judaism, under the sponsorship of the Leadership Conference, which for decades was located in the RAC's building.

The Jewish community has continued its support of civil rights laws addressing persistent discrimination in voting, housing, and employment against not only women and people of color, but also in the LGBTQ+ community and the disabled community.

5. "1994 Mugging Reveals Rosa Parks' True Character," Jeanne Theoharis, February 2, 2013, *https://womensenews.org/2013/02/1994-mugging-reveals-rosa-parks-true-character*.

6. While the decline of the Negro Leagues began as the National and American Leagues began to integrate, the East-West Game was held annually from 1933–1962. Mrs. Parks was honored by the Negro Leagues after her heroic act on December 1, 1955.

7. Rosa Parks, *My Story*, page 125.

8. *Dear Mrs. Parks,* page 63.

9. Coincidently, in 2020 *Time* magazine honored Ms. Davis as one of the most influential women of 1972. Mrs. Parks was ahead of the curve.

10. Barber, Marching on Washington (2002), p. 158. Barber, Lucy G. *Marching on Washington: The Forging of an American Political Tradition,* University of California Press, 2002.

11. *https://kinginstitute.stanford.edu/fre edom-black-women-speak-march-washington-jobs-and-freedom.*

12. "Women Were 'Second Class Citizens' at '63 March" August 28, 2013 (*www.wwno.org/2013-08-29/women-were-second-class-citizens-at-63-march*).

13. *www.history.com/this-day-in-history/mahalia-jackson-the-queen-of-gospel-puts-her-stamp-on-the-march-on-washington.*

14. *www.vatican.va/roman_curia/secretariat_state/documents/rc_seg-st_doc_20020128_martino-racism_en.html.*

## Resources Cited

Brinkley, Douglas. 2005. *Rosa Parks: A Life*. Harlow, England: Penguin Books.

McGuire, Danielle L. 2010. *At the Dark End of the Street: Black Women, Rape, and Resistance—A New History of the Civil Rights Movement from Rosa Parks to the Rise of Black Power*. Knopf Publishing Group.

Parks, Rosa. 1992. Haskins James. *Rosa Parks: My Story*. Harlow, England: Penguin Books.

_____. 1997. *Dear Mrs. Parks: A Dialogue with Today's Youth*. New York, N.Y.: Lee & Low Books.

_____. 1994. Gregory J. Reed. Quiet Strength: The Faith, the Hope, and the Heart of a Woman Who Changed a Nation. Grand Rapids, Mich.: Zondervan Publishing Company.

"Rosa Parks Collection." A gift to the Library of Congress from the Howard G. Buffett Foundation

CPSIA information can be obtained
at www.ICGtesting.com
Printed in the USA
LVHW021331290622
722241LV00005B/6